the

Goodful™

cookbook

the

Goodful™

cookbook

**SIMPLE AND BALANCED
RECIPES TO LIVE WELL**

RODALE

NEW YORK

Copyright © 2019 by BuzzFeed, Inc.

All rights reserved.
Published in the United States by Rodale Books,
an imprint of Random House, a division of
Penguin Random House LLC, New York.
rodalebooks.com

RODALE and the Plant colophon are registered
trademarks of Penguin Random House LLC.

Goodful is a trademark of BuzzFeed, Inc.
Used under license. Portions of this work originally
appeared on BuzzFeed's social media channels.

Library of Congress Cataloging-in-Publication Data is
available upon request.

ISBN 978-0-593-13549-5
Ebook ISBN 978-0-593-13550-1

Printed in Canada

Cover and book design by Jan Derevjanik
Cover and interior photographs by David Malosh

10 9 8 7 6 5 4 3 2 1

First Edition

This book is dedicated to you,
our lovely reader.

contents

welcome to *Goodful*™

We're truly thrilled to have you here. If you're already familiar with us, well then, hey! It's great to see you again. If not, it's lovely to meet you. Either way, we're so happy that you've picked up this book to learn our incredible recipes and philosophy. Goodful provides people with simple, intentional steps to live well. We exist to help you take care of yourself, your environment, and your people.

We believe in nourishment as a form of self-care. But we will never tell you what's "good" for you or the "right" way to do something. We know that nutrition means something different to every person reading this. Our cookbook is meant to give you suggestions, tips, and, of course, delicious recipes. Take this book and make it yours. Tailor everything here to your personal definition of mindfulness: leave out ingredients you're allergic to, add ingredients you love, swap out components to make a recipe more convenient. We'll guide you along the way.

We also believe in nourishment and meals as a form of connection. Use this book as a delightful excuse to meal-prep with your friends, cook dinner with your family, or provide snacks for your coworkers. Nourishing yourself and others is an incredible way to share moments with the people you care for.

Every single recipe here was created, tested, and hand selected with **you** in mind. All of your comments on our videos, direct messages, and tagged friends not only inspired this cookbook but literally created it. We dedicate this book to you, our exquisite audience.

Can't get enough of us? Connect with us online!

 facebook.com/officialgoodful   youtube.com/goodful

@goodful   goodful.com

how to use this book

Eating should be simple: Eat foods that make you feel good whenever you're hungry. There's no need to overcomplicate it (unless, of course, you're pursuing a specific diet for medical reasons and under medical supervision). There are many eating styles that can be easy to follow. For example, you may decide that a plant-based diet is what works for your body and your ethics, or you may pursue a low-carb diet because you find it fuels you best. No matter what you choose to eat, we support you. The recipes in this cookbook are about 55 percent vegetarian (with vegan options included), 45 percent meat inclusive, and 100 percent delicious. We'll always call out when a recipe conforms to a vegan, vegetarian, gluten-free, or dairy-free diet, so you'll never have to guess.

We also included nutritional information for all the recipes in this book for reference. But we don't want you to go crazy counting macros. We're all about transparency, and it's super important to us that you never have to guess what's in each dish. We understand that every body, appetite, and eating style is different! Our philosophy is simple: Use a foundation of wholesome, fresh ingredients, eat when hungry, and ultimately do what you need to do to feel **good**. No calories are bad calories, and counting them can trigger anxiety. That said, we tried to keep every recipe under 700 calories per serving (with a few exceptions), maintaining a balance of fat, carbohydrates, protein, fiber, and sugar.

We also did our best to call for ingredients that can be found in most grocery stores so that all of our recipes are accessible to everyone. We sometimes use less common ingredients to accommodate alternative diets, but these are always optional and can be swapped out for other ingredients of your choosing. *And* since we know you're busy, we made sure these recipes are simple enough to make but don't sacrifice flavor—so you aren't spending all day in the kitchen (unless you want to!).

We're all for great store-bought shortcuts to help make life easier too. Pre-made cauliflower rice, refrigerated hummus, frozen veggies, peeled and deveined shrimp, low-sodium stock and bone broths, and instant cooked brown rice (just to name a few) are amazing time-saving ingredients. It's totally okay to use these whenever you want. We know that it's not always feasible to make everything from scratch.

Use our recipes as inspirations for new dishes to accommodate your (and your loved ones') tastes. Feel free to take notes in the margins, leave out ingredients you don't like, or add your own favorites. Mix and match according to your preferences and what works for you and your body. It's really about choosing and modifying so that everything works for **you**.

We believe that one of the keys to wellness is what you put in your body. Each ingredient here was added with a sense of purpose to help balance nutrition and with your busy life in mind. Of course, food is also about celebration and pleasure, so we made sure every recipe is delicious. Enjoy!

how to stock your kitchen

A well-stocked, well-thought-out kitchen is a great step toward meals that make you feel good. Having a variety of herbs, spices, and other ingredients on hand will provide so many options for simple yet tasty dishes on those whirlwind days when delivery beckons. An added perk? These pantry items often pack a surprising nutritional punch. Here is a list of versatile staple ingredients that build a foundation for easy, nutritious cooking. Next time you head to the store, use this list as a guide, tailor it to your preferences, and make a mental note whenever you're running low on anything (or keep a checklist; we love checklists).

FLOURS

All-purpose

Whole-wheat

Almond flour

Buckwheat flour

Coconut flour

BAKING PRODUCTS

Agave nectar

Baking powder

Baking soda

Organic sugar

Pure vanilla extract

Quick oats and old-fashioned rolled oats

Raw honey

CONDIMENTS

Chili paste

Dijon mustard

Hot sauce

Ketchup

Mayonnaise

Oils: canola, extra-virgin olive (EVOO), avocado

Soy sauce

Vinegars: balsamic, cider, distilled red wine, rice wine, white

Worcestershire sauce

SEASONINGS

Black peppercorns

Chili powder

Dried herbs and
spices: allspice,
bay leaves, cayenne
pepper, cinnamon,
cloves, crushed red
pepper, cumin, ground
coriander, ground
ginger, nutmeg,
oregano, paprika,
rosemary, thyme

Italian seasoning

Kosher salt

Nutritional yeast

CANNED GOODS

Beans: black, cannellini,
chickpeas, kidney

Canned tomatoes

Fruit preserves or jelly

Low-sodium stock
or broth

Olives

Salsa

Tomato paste

Tuna fish

GRAINS AND LEGUMES

Brown rice

Couscous

Pasta: regular,
whole-wheat, lentil

Quinoa

REFRIGERATOR ESSENTIALS

Almond milk

Almond milk yogurt

Cashew milk

Cheeses of your
choosing (there are
dairy-free options in
many markets)

Coconut milk

Coconut milk yogurt

Corn tortillas

Feta

Free-range large eggs

Grass-fed organic
butter or ghee

Greek yogurt

Kefir

Mozzarella

Organic cow's milk

Parmesan

Rice milk

FREEZER ESSENTIALS

Fruit: blackberries,
blueberries, peaches,
strawberries

Vegetables: broccoli,
corn, edamame, peas,
spinach

PRODUCE ESSENTIALS

Garlic

Greens: arugula , kale,
romaine, spinach

Onions: red,
yellow

Sweet potatoes

NUTS, NUT BUTTERS, SEEDS, AND DRIED FRUIT

Almonds

Dried apricots

Dried cranberries

Chia seeds

Natural almond butter

Natural peanut butter

Raisins

Sesame seeds: white,
black

Tahini

Walnuts

food lifestyles

Goodful is a judgment-free friend when it comes to finding the style of eating that supports your body, your happiness, and your belief system. There's no one right way to eat, but there are a few general principles that underlie any nutritious lifestyle: Use ingredients that are as unprocessed, fresh, and wholesome as possible (for you, that may mean organic), make what you can from scratch, and practice balance and moderation without depriving yourself. Remember: This is about feeling good! If a style of eating makes you feel hungry, lightheaded, or obsessive, that's a sign it's not working for you.

You may find it helpful to follow one of the popular eating styles listed here. When a recipe in this book aligns with one of them, it will be marked with the symbol below.

V Vegan   GF Gluten-Free

VG Vegetarian   DF Dairy-Free

Vegetarian

A vegetarian is someone who does not eat meat, game, fish, poultry, shellfish, or products with ingredients derived from animals. People decide to be a vegetarian for many reasons, including animal rights, ethics, health, environmentalism, and religion. Vegetarian diets include fruits, vegetables, grains, nuts, and seeds. Dairy and eggs may be included, depending on the type of diet one follows.

Vegetarianism has been linked to lower cholesterol and decreased blood pressure.

Types of vegetarians include:

Lacto-ovo vegetarians: Vegetarians who do not eat animal flesh but do eat dairy and egg products.

Lacto-vegetarians: Vegetarians who avoid animal flesh and eggs but consume dairy products.

Ovo-vegetarians: Vegetarians who avoid animal flesh and dairy products but eat eggs.

Flexitarians: Part-time vegetarians.

Pescatarians: Those who avoid meat and poultry but eat fish.

Vegan

A vegan lifestyle is defined by the Vegan Society as a way of living that attempts to exclude all forms of animal exploitation and cruelty as much as possible.

This means a vegan diet not only eliminates animal flesh but also dairy, eggs, and animal-derived ingredients. These include honey, pepsin, gelatin, carmine, whey, albumin, casein, and some forms of vitamin D3. Vegans avoid all animal by-products. Many vegans believe that animals shouldn't be used by humans for the purposes of clothing, food, science, and entertainment. Their environmental concerns may include the fact that raising animals for food generates greenhouse gases, which contribute to global warming; requires more water than farming crops; and pollutes our waterways with animal waste, antibiotics, and hormones.

Keto

The keto diet focuses on fats supplying up to 90 percent of daily calories. This creates ketone bodies, a type of fuel that the liver produces from stored fat. The goal in keto eating is to have your body reach a state of ketosis. To do so, carbohydrate intake is decreased to less than 20 to 50 grams per day.

All types of fats and proteins are allowed on the keto diet, as are some fruits and vegetables. Typical meals include a mushroom omelet; a salad with hard-boiled eggs, cheese, turkey, and avocado; and pork chops with low-carbohydrate vegetables. Keto followers say they have increased energy and focus.

Low Carb

A low-carb diet cuts out carbohydrates such as grains, starchy vegetables, and fruit. Protein and fat are the main macronutrients included in meals. People often follow low-carb diets to control their blood sugar, especially if they have diabetes. Meals may include vegetarian proteins, meat, poultry, fish, and eggs, along with vegetables. A typical daily limit of carbohydrates is 20 to 60 grams (in comparison, the average American diet consists of 250 grams of carbohydrates per day). Those who follow a low-carb lifestyle should choose foods with healthy unsaturated fats and lean proteins. People often say that they have more energy with a low-carb diet.

Dairy-Free

People follow a dairy-free diet for various reasons, often due to digestive issues, bloating, skin problems, and respiratory conditions that are caused by eating dairy products.

A dairy-free diet eliminates foods that contain milk and milk products. People who are lactose intolerant will reduce or eliminate foods that contain lactose. Those allergic to milk avoid its proteins and find alternatives such as oat milk, almond milk, or coconut milk; cheese made from soy or nuts like cashews; and yogurt made with almond, soy, or coconut milk.

The sources of dairy to avoid when following a dairy-free diet include milk, cheese, cream cheese, butter, sour cream, cottage cheese, custards and puddings, ice cream, gelato, sherbet, and products that include whey and casein.

food and physical health

You truly are what you eat. Food can affect everything from your energy levels, skin, and hair to your overall quality of life. Eating a balanced diet nourishes your body with what it needs to thrive (this means something different for every body). The amounts of protein, carbs, fat, and vitamins in food can affect your physical health; these all help to protect your body from anything that comes its way.

Balancing each of these nutrients can provide your body with what it needs to take on the world. Proteins help your body build muscle and keep your immune system strong.

Excellent sources of protein are lean meat, poultry, fish, dairy products, nuts, beans, peas, and lentils. Carbs are your body's main source of energy. These are mostly found in bread, pasta, grains, fruits, and starchy vegetables. Fats give your body the amino acids it needs to produce cells and can also be reserved for energy. There are different types of fats found in all kinds of different foods (both in plant- and animal-based foods). Finally, there are an array of vitamins that all have potential benefits for the maintenance of bodily processes.

food and mood

Believe it or not, food has a big impact on the brain. Your brain works 24/7, never taking a break, even when you're asleep! Serotonin is a hormone in the brain known as the happy chemical because it calms and uplifts you. Sounds amazing, right? Even more amazing: some foods, such as turkey, eggs, cheese, and bananas are known to raise your serotonin levels.

Another way to improve your mood is to be mindful of your sugar intake. A sweet treat here and there is fine, but a diet loaded with refined sugars can make a bad mood worse. In addition, skipping meals, especially breakfast may cause low blood sugar, which can make you cranky.

Try these mood-boosting foods:

Berries: Blueberries, raspberries, and strawberries are high in vitamin C, which helps lower cortisol, a hormone that is released during times of stress.

Dark chocolate: Chocolate causes the brain to release dopamine, which supports a positive mood.

Herbal teas: Many herbal teas, such as chamomile, have calming properties. Black, green, white, and red rooibos teas are also rich in antioxidants. Drink a cup of warm tea to relieve stress and lift your spirits.

Beans: Black beans, lima beans, and lentils are loaded with magnesium, a mineral that helps with relaxation and calmness.

Fish: Mackerel, sardines, salmon, and trout contain omega-3 fatty acids, which can reduce anxiety.

food and sustainability

Sustainability emphasizes food that is grown in a way that protects our planet. Sustainability includes how food is produced, how it's distributed, and how it's consumed. When buying an ingredient, it's important to take into consideration its environmental impact, resource usage, and agricultural practices.

Sustainable farming practices use organic and low-carbon food production. Organic produce and organic ingredients are grown without pesticides, synthetic fertilizers, sewage sludge, genetically modified organisms, or ionizing radiation. Animals that produce organic meat, poultry, eggs, and dairy products are not given antibiotics or growth hormones.

When choosing ingredients, look for farmers who treat animals with care and use livestock techniques that protect the animals' well-being. There are many ways to find these types of products. Look for the CERTIFIED HUMANE RAISED AND HANDLED or CERTIFIED HUMANE labels, which indicate that the food products have come from facilities that meet precise, objective standards for farm animal treatment. Another certification to look for is CERTIFIED ANIMAL WELFARE APPROVED by A Greener World (AWA), an independent, non-profit farm certification program.

Other tips for finding sustainable products include buying organic (look for CERTIFIED ORGANIC or CERTIFIED NATURALLY GROWN labels), shopping at farmers' markets, and looking for food cooperatives. These are businesses that offer fresh, locally grown food at reasonable prices because the purpose of a co-op is not to make a profit but to meet the needs of its members. Don't forget your reusable shopping bags!

what's in season?

WINTER

Apples
Avocados
Bananas
Beets
Brussels Sprouts
Cabbage
Carrots
Celery
Collard Greens
Grapefruit
Kale
Kiwifruit
Leeks
Lemons

Limes
Onions
Oranges
Parsnips
Pears
Pineapples
Potatoes
Pumpkin
Rutabagas
Sweet Potatoes and Yams
Swiss Chard
Turnips
Winter Squash

SPRING

Apples
Apricots
Asparagus
Avocados
Bananas
Broccoli
Cabbage
Carrots
Celery
Collard Greens
Garlic
Kale
Kiwifruit

Lemons
Lettuce
Limes
Mushrooms
Onions
Peas
Pineapples
Radishes
Rhubarb
Spinach
Strawberries
Swiss Chard
Turnips

SUMMER

Apples
Apricots
Avocados
Bananas
Beets
Bell Peppers
Blackberries
Blueberries
Cantaloupe
Carrots
Celery
Cherries
Corn
Cucumbers
Eggplant
Garlic

Green Beans
Honeydew Melon
Lemons
Lima Beans
Limes
Mangoes
Okra
Peaches
Plums
Raspberries
Strawberries
Summer Squash
Tomatillos
Tomatoes
Watermelon
Zucchini

FALL

Apples
Bananas
Beets
Bell Peppers
Broccoli
Brussels Sprouts
Cabbage
Carrots
Cauliflower
Celery
Collard Greens
Cranberries
Garlic
Ginger
Grapes
Green Beans
Kale
Kiwifruit
Lemons
Lettuce

Limes
Mangoes
Mushrooms
Onions
Parsnips
Pears
Peas
Pineapples
Potatoes
Pumpkin
Radishes
Raspberries
Rutabagas
Spinach
Sweet Potatoes and Yams
Swiss Chard
Turnips
Winter Squash

food storage

Ever wonder if that cilantro in your fridge is still okay to eat? How long does an avocado last? Having a good understanding of food storage is important to reduce food waste and get the most out of your groceries. The number one thing to remember is to refrigerate or freeze perishables immediately. Remember the "two-hour rule" for items that need refrigeration—that's how long they can sit out at room temperature. The refrigerator temperature should be kept at or below 40°F (4°C). The freezer temperature should be 0°F (–18°C). Here are some tips for storing common foods:

Fruits: Bananas, melons, and citrus are best when left on the counter. Once they are cut, place them in the fridge.

Garlic, onions, and shallots: Store in a cool, dry place for up to two weeks. In the fridge, they will lose their flavor.

Tomatoes: Store unripe green tomatoes stem-side down in a paper bag or in a cardboard box in a single layer. Keep in a cool area until they are ripe. Ripe tomatoes should be kept at room temperature on the counter away from sunlight. Arrange them in a single layer, not touching one another, and stem-side up. Overripe tomatoes can be placed in the refrigerator. The cold air will prevent the tomatoes from ripening more.

Potatoes: Do not store potatoes in the refrigerator. Put potatoes in a well-ventilated container and store in a dry location, away from sunlight, in the coolest part of the kitchen. Do not store in a plastic bag or closed container, as this will create moisture.

Bread: Store bread at room temperature for up to two days, either tightly wrapped in foil or in a zip-top plastic storage bag to limit loss of moisture. After two days, wrap the bread in foil, put it into a freezer bag, and freeze it.

Cakes and pies: Cakes and pies will last for about a week when tightly wrapped in cling wrap. Cut cakes and pies last three to four days. Cream-based pies or pies containing eggs, such as custard, should be stored, loosely covered, in the refrigerator.

Dry goods: Dry goods can be stored for up to six months. After opening the box or package, store the ingredient in an airtight container.

Nuts: Nuts should be kept in airtight containers. This allows them to maintain the right level of moisture. Place the containers in the refrigerator or the freezer; they will stay fresh for up to six months in the refrigerator and up to one year in the freezer.

Spices: Heat, light, air, and humidity are all bad for spices. Airtight tins or spice jars are best. Whole spices can be kept for up to two years, while ground spices should be refreshed every six months.

Eggs: Eggs are best kept in their original carton on a shelf in the refrigerator. Eggs should not be stored in the refrigerator door but in the body of the refrigerator to ensure that they are kept at a consistent, cool temperature. The carton protects the eggs and they will not absorb odors and flavors of other foods in your refrigerator.

Dairy products: Cream, milk, yogurt, and other dairy products should be stored on the upper shelves of your refrigerator. The temperature there is the most consistent. Cheese should be wrapped in porous material. Cheese paper is ideal, but waxed paper or parchment paper will also work. Before storing, scrape the cheese's surface with a non-serrated knife to remove excess oil that may have appeared when at room temperature.

Vegetables: All vegetables, except those that can be stored at room temperature, should be stored in bags in your refrigerator's crisper drawer. Keep them separate from fruit.

Fruit: All fruit except melons, citrus, and bananas should be stored in the refrigerator in a separate drawer from the vegetables. Do not wash your fruit until you are ready to eat it.

Meat: Meat should be placed in the coldest part of the refrigerator: the bottom. Use refrigerated meat within four days of purchase. Freeze uncooked meat in its original packaging. According to the USDA, the maximum recommended freezer storage time for beef and lamb is six months; for veal, pork, and poultry, four months.

Fish: Dry it completely and wrap it in waxed paper before refrigerating. It will keep in the coldest part of your refrigerator for up to two days, but if it smells too fishy or has an unusual color, throw it out. Fish can last in the freezer for up to six months.

Fresh herbs: Basil, parsley, cilantro, and other leafy herbs should be treated like flowers. Remove twisty ties, trim a small amount off the stem ends, and place the bunch into a jar or glass of water. Keep the herbs in the water, and place it on your kitchen counter or in the refrigerator.

Stock: Freeze stock in ice cube trays or muffin tins until solid, then store the cubes/chunks in a freezer bag. You can use these small amounts of stock whenever you need them. Frozen stock will last for up to two months.

Coffee: Store in a dry, airtight container. Keep the container in a location that will not expose the coffee to air, moisture, heat, or light. Stored this way, it should stay fresh for one to two weeks.

Don't forget to check expiration dates! A "use-by" date means that the manufacturer recommends using the product by this date for the best flavor or quality. However, the date is not a food safety date. After the use-by date, a product may change in taste, color, texture, or nutrient content, but it may be safe to eat after that date. Always toss anything that looks or smells bad.

more of this	less of that
sweet potatoes	white potatoes
Greek yogurt	regular yogurt
quinoa and brown rice	white rice
salmon	red meat
avocado	cheese
nuts	chips
olive oil	butter
oats	cornflakes
bone broth	dehydrated soups
spices	salt
dark chocolate	milk chocolate
fresh fruit	sugary juices
corn/whole-wheat tortillas	flour tortillas
whole-grain bread	white bread
baked/grilled/steamed foods	fried foods

cooking conversions

	CUPS	TABLESPOONS	OUNCES	GRAMS
BUTTER	¼ cup	4 Tbsp	2oz	57g
	⅓ cup	5 Tbsp + 1 tsp	2.67oz	76g
	1 cup	16 Tbsp	8oz	220g
FLOUR (SIFTED)	¼ cup	4 Tbsp	1oz	30g
	⅓ cup	5 Tbsp + 1 tsp	1.5oz	40g
	½ cup	8 Tbsp	2.25oz	60g
	1 cup	16 Tbsp	4.25oz	120g
GRANULATED SUGAR	¼ cup	4 Tbsp	1.75oz	50g
	⅓ cup	5 Tbsp + 1 tsp	2.29oz	65g
	½ cup	8 Tbsp	3.5oz	100g
	1 cup	16 Tbsp	7oz	200g
BROWN SUGAR (LIGHTLY PACKED)	¼ cup	4 Tbsp	1.59oz	50g
	⅓ cup	5 Tbsp + 1 tsp	2.12oz	65g
	½ cup	8 Tbsp	3.2oz	100g
	1 cup	16 Tbsp	6.4oz	200g
WATER	¼ cup	4 Tbsp	2oz	60ml
	⅓ cup	5 Tbsp + 1 tsp	2.67oz	80ml
	½ cup	8 Tbsp	4oz	120ml
	1 cup	16 Tbsp	8oz	240ml

1 tablespoon = 3 teaspoons

4 tablespoons = ¼ cup

1 cup = 240ml

1 pint = 475ml

1 quart = 950ml

1 gallon = 3.8L

1 ounce = 30g

4 ounces or ¼ pound = 115g

⅓ pound = 150g

8 ounces or ½ pound = 225g

⅔ pound = 300g

12 ounces or ¾ pound = 340g

1 pound or 16 ounces = 450g

2 pounds = 900g

1 teaspoon = 5ml

1 tablespoon or ½ fluid ounce = 15ml

1 fluid ounce or ⅛ cup = 30ml

¼ cup or 2 fluid ounces = 60ml

⅓ cup = 80ml

½ cup or 4 fluid ounces = 120ml

⅔ cup = 160ml

¾ cup or 6 fluid ounces = 175ml

1 cup or 8 fluid ounces or half a pint = 240ml

2 cups or 1 pint or 16 fluid ounces = 475ml

4 cups or 2 pints or 1 quart = 950ml

4 quarts or 1 gallon = 3.8L

mornings

"

Spending just a few minutes thinking positive thoughts is a great way to start the day.

"

good morning

Some of our breakfast recipes are super quick to get you out the door and travel with you on the go, while others are perfect for batch cooking or hosting brunches with friends.

"cheesy" vegan breakfast tacos

FOR 1 SERVING

Ready to break up with your cereal or oatmeal routine? If so, these tofu tacos are hearty, veggie-packed, and filling. They are perfectly portioned for one but easy to double or triple if you have company. The secret ingredient, nutritional yeast, adds a savory, cheesy flavor and gives you a boost of protein and energizing B_{12}.

1 tablespoon extra-virgin olive oil

⅓ block firm tofu, about 4½ ounces, patted dry

1 tablespoon low-sodium soy sauce

1 tablespoon nutritional yeast

½ teaspoon ground turmeric

¾ teaspoon garlic powder

Freshly ground black pepper

¼ red bell pepper, diced (about ¼ cup)

1 cup lightly packed baby spinach

1 (8-inch) whole-wheat tortilla

¼ avocado, sliced

Hot sauce (optional)

1. In a 9-inch nonstick sauté pan or cast-iron skillet, heat the oil over medium-high. Add the tofu and break it up with a spoon into small curds. Sauté until lightly browned, 4 to 6 minutes.

2. Add the soy sauce, nutritional yeast, turmeric, garlic powder, black pepper, bell pepper, and spinach, and sauté until the spinach is wilted and the bell pepper is just softened, 3 to 4 minutes. Transfer the tofu mixture to a plate and set aside.

3. In the same pan (carefully wipe it clean if needed), heat the tortilla for 15 to 20 seconds on each side.

4. Remove the tortilla from the pan and serve it topped with the tofu mixture, avocado, and hot sauce, if using.

NUTRITION

| Calories: 575 | Carbs: 49 grams | Fiber: 15 grams |
| Fat: 33 grams | Protein: 28 grams | Sugar: 5 grams |

cauliflower-crusted feta-and-asparagus quiche

FOR 8 SERVINGS

This delectable quiche uses a cauliflower crust to keep it light, gluten-free, kosher, and low in carbs. Loaded with protein-packed eggs, iron-rich spinach, and fiber-filled cauliflower, this cheesy, crispy dish is a satisfying breakfast, brunch, or even lunch. This stores great as leftovers for an easy morning meal.

1 head cauliflower, cut into florets (about 7 cups)

6 large free-range eggs

½ cup grated Parmesan cheese

¼ teaspoon garlic powder

¾ teaspoon kosher salt

Nonstick cooking spray

½ cup whole milk

½ cup crumbled feta cheese, about 2¾ ounces

½ teaspoon freshly ground black pepper

1½ teaspoons extra-virgin olive oil

8 medium spears asparagus, trimmed and cut into 1-inch pieces (about 1 cup)

4 cups baby spinach, about 4 ounces

4 scallions, chopped (about ⅓ cup)

1. Preheat the oven to 425°F.

2. Place the cauliflower in a food processor and pulse until finely crumbled. Transfer to a microwave-safe dish and microwave on high for 5 minutes. Let cool completely.

3. Place the cooked cauliflower in a clean kitchen towel and squeeze out as much water as possible. In a large bowl, combine the cauliflower, 1 egg, the Parmesan, garlic powder, and ¼ teaspoon of the salt.

4. Liberally spray a 9-inch tart pan with sides about 1 inch tall with nonstick cooking spray. Press the cauliflower mixture firmly into the pan, making sure to go up the sides of the pan. Place the tart pan on a baking sheet and bake until lightly golden around the edges, about 15 minutes. Set aside to cool.

5. Reduce the oven temperature to 375°F.

6. In a large bowl, whisk together the remaining 5 eggs, the milk, feta, remaining ½ teaspoon salt, and the pepper.

7. In a medium skillet, heat the oil over medium heat until shimmering. Add the asparagus and cook until slightly tender, 2 to 3 minutes. Add the spinach and cook until wilted, 1 to 2 minutes.

8. Spread the asparagus mixture onto the cooked cauliflower crust. Pour the egg mixture over the asparagus mixture. Sprinkle the scallions over the top.

9. Bake until the quiche is puffed and just set, 35 to 45 minutes.

10. Let cool for 15 minutes before serving.

NUTRITION, per serving

Calories: 171	Carbs: 10 grams	Fiber: 1 grams
Fat: 10 grams	Protein: 13 grams	Sugar: 4 grams

chewy chocolate cranberry breakfast bars

(V) (GF)

FOR 8 SERVINGS

Need a balanced breakfast to take with you on the go? These bars are perfect to grab in a pinch for your morning commute. They're also super easy to make ahead of time as part of your Sunday meal prep. Filled with almond butter and oats, they'll give you long-lasting energy. And the best part? Dark chocolate is not just a treat; it's high in minerals and antioxidants, and can reduce the risk of heart disease.

Coconut oil, for greasing the pan

1 cup almond butter, about 9½ ounces

½ cup maple syrup

½ cup almond milk

1 teaspoon pure vanilla extract

2½ cups rolled oats

1 cup brown rice cereal

½ cup sliced almonds

⅓ cup dried cranberries

⅓ cup dark chocolate chunks, about 2½ ounces

¼ cup dark chocolate chunks, about 1¼ ounces, melted

1. Preheat the oven to 325°F. Line an 8 × 8-inch baking pan with parchment paper and grease it with coconut oil.

2. In a large bowl, combine the almond butter, maple syrup, almond milk, and vanilla. Stir or whisk until smooth.

3. Add the oats, brown rice cereal, almonds, cranberries, and the ⅓ cup dark chocolate chunks. Stir to combine.

4. Transfer the mixture to the prepared pan. Firmly press down on the mixture until it is one smooth layer. Grease a spatula and use it to pack down the mixture even more.

5. Bake until light golden brown around the edges and the top is dry and tacky, about 20 minutes. Let cool for 10 minutes.

6. Drizzle the granola with the melted chocolate and chill in the refrigerator until set, 30 to 45 minutes. If the chocolate is not set after 45 minutes, place the bars in the freezer for about 10 minutes.

7. Cut the granola into 8 equal pieces. Wrap each bar in parchment paper or reusable beeswax wrap and store in the refrigerator for up to 1 week or in the freezer for up to 3 months.

NUTRITION, per serving

| Calories: 421 | Carbs: 40 grams | Fiber: 6 grams |
| Fat: 27 grams | Protein: 10 grams | Sugar: 23 grams |

brunch lox on everything flatbread

FOR 4 SERVINGS

This is our nutritious take on another classic brunch dish! The lighter cream cheese substitute contains more protein and fewer calories than traditional cream cheese but still has that savory, cheesy creamy taste you crave. Might we also add that the Everything Seasoning is good on everything: avocado toast, popcorn, scrambled eggs—you name it. This will be a definite crowd-pleaser, so it's a great choice to pair with a bright cup of orange juice (or even a mimosa) the next time friends are coming over for brunch.

LIGHTER CREAM CHEESE

½ cup 4% cottage cheese, about 4½ ounces

½ cup full-fat Greek yogurt, about 4 ounces

⅛ teaspoon kosher salt

One 9 × 12-inch plain lavash

Olive oil spray

EVERYTHING SEASONING

2 tablespoons poppy seeds

1 tablespoon white sesame seeds

1 tablespoon black sesame seeds

1 tablespoon dried minced garlic

1 tablespoon dried minced onion

1 tablespoon flaked sea salt

LOX

8 ounces lox or smoked salmon

¼ small red onion, thinly sliced (about ⅓ cup)

2 tablespoons capers

2 tablespoons roughly chopped fresh dill

½ lemon, cut into wedges

1. The night before serving, add the cottage cheese, Greek yogurt, and salt to a blender. Turn it on low and slowly increase the speed to ensure the mixture blends evenly. Blend until completely smooth. Over a medium bowl, line a fine sieve with cheesecloth or two layers of paper towels and add the "cream cheese." Let it strain in the refrigerator overnight.

2. The following morning, preheat the oven to 350°F. Line a baking sheet with a reusable baking mat or parchment paper.

3. Lightly grease both sides of the lavash with the oil spray. Bake until the lavash is crisped to your liking, 5 to 7 minutes. Set aside to cool.

4. In a jar with a tight-fitting lid, add the poppy seeds, sesame seeds, garlic, onion, and salt. Close the lid and shake to combine. This seasoning mix will last for up to 6 months in a cool, dry place.

5. Spread the lighter cream cheese over the lavash. Layer on the lox, red onion, and capers. Sprinkle the dill and some everything seasoning over the top. Slice in half lengthwise and then cut into skinny triangles. Serve with lemon wedges and extra everything seasoning.

NUTRITION, per serving

Calories: 241	Carbs: 19 grams	Fiber: 2 grams
Fat: 9 grams	Protein: 20 grams	Sugar: 3 grams

better instant oatmeal
plain for meal prepping

FOR 10 SERVINGS

This is a breakfast classic with a modern and convenient meal-prep twist. This recipe makes ten servings of dry oatmeal, which you can store in a cool, dry place for up to a month in an eight-cup (64-ounce) airtight container with your favorite fruit-and-nut combo already mixed in. (Blueberry Almond and Banana Bread are included here—or come up with your own!) When you're ready to eat, just scoop out ½ cup and combine with boiling water for a morning made easy!

DRY OATMEAL MIX

6 cups rolled oats, about 1¼ pounds

½ teaspoon kosher salt

FOR 1 SERVING

¾ cup whole milk or water, boiling, plus more if needed

1. Place the oats in a large bowl.

2. Scoop 2 cups of the oats into a blender or food processor and blend until it becomes a fine powder.

3. Combine the blended oats with the whole rolled oats. Add the salt and stir until evenly combined. (This makes about 5 cups plain instant oatmeal.)

4. Stir in your desired flavor additions and transfer the instant oatmeal mixture to an 8-cup airtight container or divide it into ten ½-cup airtight containers for single-serve portions.

5. When ready to eat, pour the boiling milk over the oatmeal mixture and stir to combine. Let sit for about 3 minutes. Stir in additional boiling milk if needed to reach your desired consistency.

NUTRITION, per ½ cup dry oatmeal

Calories: 27	Carbs: 4 grams	Fiber: 0 grams
Fat: 1 gram	Protein: 1 gram	Sugar: 1 gram

blueberry almond

FOR 1 SERVING

½ cup Better Instant Oatmeal, about 2¾ ounces

2 tablespoons freeze-dried blueberries

1 tablespoon sliced almonds, plus more for topping

1 teaspoon chia seeds

Seeds from ¼ vanilla bean

2 teaspoons sweetener of choice

¾ cup whole milk or water, boiling, plus more if needed

Fresh blueberries, for topping

1. In a mason jar, combine the instant oatmeal, blueberries, almonds, chia seeds, vanilla seeds, and sweetener.

2. If not using immediately, store in a cool, dry place for up to 1 month.

3. To prepare, pour the boiling milk over the oats in the mason jar. Stir to combine and let sit for about 3 minutes. Stir in additional boiling milk if needed to reach your desired consistency.

4. Serve with sliced almonds and fresh blueberries sprinkled over top.

NUTRITION

| Calories: 269 | Carbs: 32 grams | Fiber: 4 grams |
| Fat: 12 grams | Protein: 10 grams | Sugar: 20 grams |

banana bread instant oatmeal

FOR 1 SERVING

½ cup Better Instant Oatmeal, about 2¾ ounces

3 tablespoons chopped freeze-dried bananas

1 tablespoon chopped walnuts, plus more for topping

Seeds from ¼ vanilla bean

2 teaspoons sweetener of choice

¾ cup whole milk or water, boiling, plus more if needed

Sliced fresh banana, for topping

1. In a mason jar, combine the instant oatmeal, bananas, walnuts, vanilla seeds, and sweetener.

2. If not using immediately, store in a cool, dry place for up to 1 month.

3. To prepare, pour the boiling milk over the oats in the mason jar. Stir to combine and let sit for about 3 minutes. Stir in additional boiling milk if needed to reach your desired consistency.

4. Serve with chopped walnuts and sliced banana over top.

NUTRITION

| Calories: 378 | Carbs: 54 grams | Fiber: 6 grams |
| Fat: 14 grams | Protein: 13 grams | Sugar: 23 grams |

avocado egg cups
with roasted red pepper sauce

Why cook eggs in a pan when you can bake them inside cute avocado cups? This tangy red pepper sauce, similar to a romesco sauce, will really kick your breakfast up a notch. You can refrigerate the sauce in an airtight container for up to one week, or freeze it for up to three months. Feel free to use it on other dishes for an extra flavor punch too! If red pepper is not your thing, sprinkle the eggs with cheese and top with salsa or your favorite tomato sauce.

AVOCADO CUPS

2 large avocados

4 medium free-range eggs

Kosher salt and freshly ground black pepper

ROASTED RED PEPPER SAUCE

8 ounces roasted red peppers (about 1 cup), drained, liquid reserved

2 tablespoons red wine vinegar

2 tablespoons raw almonds, about 1 ounce

½ small shallot, roughly chopped (about 1 heaping tablespoon)

1 garlic clove

Pinch of kosher salt

¼ cup extra-virgin olive oil

2 chives, finely chopped, for garnish

1. Preheat the oven to 400°F.

2. Slice the avocados in half and remove the pits.

3. Scoop some of the flesh out of each avocado half to make room for the eggs. Place the avocado halves on a small baking dish or rimmed baking sheet with the holes facing up. Rest the avocados on the sides of the dish or baking sheet so that they sit upright.

4. Crack one egg into each hole and season with salt and pepper. If the eggs are too large, break them into a fine-mesh sieve over a bowl to catch the most watery bit of the egg. Pour the thicker part of the white and the yolk into the hole.

5. Bake until the whites are set and the yolks reach your desired consistency, about 15 minutes for a runny yolk, 18 minutes for set.

6. Meanwhile, make the roasted red pepper sauce. In a blender, combine the peppers, vinegar, almonds, shallot, garlic, and salt. Blend until smooth, 30 to 45 seconds. With the blender running, slowly add the olive oil to emulsify the sauce. Thin with the reserved red pepper liquid, if necessary.

7. Drizzle the red pepper sauce over the avocado eggs and top with the fresh chives.

TIP

Running eggs through a fine-mesh sieve over a bowl is also great for poaching eggs. The stringy bits will be strained out along with the watery parts.

NUTRITION, per avocado egg cup

| Calories: 187 | Carbs: 7 grams | Fiber: 5 grams |
| Fat: 15 grams | Protein: 8 grams | Sugar: 0 grams |

NUTRITION, per 2 tablespoons roasted red pepper sauce

| Calories: 175 | Carbs: 6 grams | Fiber: 1 gram |
| Fat: 17 grams | Protein: 1 gram | Sugar: 3 grams |

grapefruit yogurt
with coconut muesli

FOR 2 SERVINGS

Level up your yogurt with a bright grapefruit twist! Grapefruits are high in vitamins A and C, which keep your immune system strong. Make the muesli ahead of time so you can scoop out ½ cup every time you crave it.

YOGURT

1 large ruby red grapefruit, about 1¼ pounds

1 cup full-fat plain Greek yogurt

1 tablespoon raw honey, plus more for drizzling, if desired

Kosher salt

MUESLI (MAKES ABOUT 6 CUPS)

3 cups rolled oats (not steel-cut or instant)

1 cup rice puffs or quinoa puffs

½ cup unsweetened coconut flakes

½ cup slivered almonds

½ cup raw pepitas (pumpkin seeds)

¾ cup dried sour cherries or dried fruit of your choosing

3 tablespoons chia seeds

1 teaspoon cinnamon

¼ teaspoon kosher salt

Fresh mint leaves, for garnish (optional)

1. Cut the two ends off the grapefruit. Stand it on one cut side on a work surface and slice from top to bottom following the natural shape of the grapefruit to remove the pith and peel.

2. Over a small bowl to catch the juices, hold the grapefruit in one hand and, with a paring knife, make a "V" along the membrane to remove the segments of the fruit. Cut to the middle of the fruit without going all the way through the center. When you reach the middle of the grapefruit, don't cut through any of the membrane. Once you remove a fruit segment, place it in the bowl with the juices. Once finished removing all the fruit, squeeze the leftover membrane over the bowl to get the juice out of the fruit.

3. In a small bowl, combine the yogurt, honey, and a pinch of salt. Pour ¼ cup of the grapefruit juice over top and stir to combine.

4. In a large airtight container, combine the oats, rice puffs, coconut flakes, almonds, pepitas, dried cherries, chia seeds, cinnamon, and salt. Close and shake to evenly mix the muesli. It will keep for up to 6 months in the container.

5. To serve, add half the yogurt to a bowl, sprinkle with ½ cup of the muesli, lay a few grapefruit slices on top, drizzle with additional honey, and garnish with mint (if using). Any unused yogurt will keep in an airtight container in the refrigerator for up to 3 days.

NUTRITION, muesli, per ½-cup serving

Calories: 173	Carbs: 23 grams	Fiber: 5 grams
Fat: 7 grams	Protein: 5 grams	Sugar: 1 gram

NUTRITION, yogurt, per ½-cup serving

Calories: 237	Carbs: 37 grams	Fiber: 4 grams
Fat: 6 grams	Protein: 12 grams	Sugar: 29 grams

NUTRITION, per serving of yogurt and muesli

Calories: 410	Carbs: 60	Fiber: 9 grams
Fat: 13 grams	Protein: 17 grams	Sugar: 30 grams

paleo almond coconut pancakes
with date syrup

FOR 3 SERVINGS

These rustic pancakes are perfect for a rainy morning in with your besties or for a sunny, lazy brunch in the backyard. And yes, they're paleo, meaning there's no wheat or dairy. The dates make a mineral-rich sweet syrup. Plus, these pancakes are a great way to use up overripe bananas. The natural sugars of the dates and bananas are all you need for a heavenly sweet breakfast.

DATE SYRUP

1 cup pitted dates

2 teaspoons freshly squeezed lemon juice

⅛ teaspoon kosher salt

1¾ cups just-boiled water, plus more to thin, if desired

PANCAKES

3 large free-range eggs

1 ripe banana, smashed (⅓ cup)

1¾ cups unsweetened almond milk or milk of choice, plus 1 to 2 tablespoons if needed

2 tablespoons avocado oil or vegetable oil, plus more for cooking

1 teaspoon pure vanilla extract

1 cup packed superfine almond flour, about 4 ounces

¼ cup packed coconut flour, about 1 ounce

1½ teaspoons baking powder

¼ teaspoon fine sea salt

¼ teaspoon cinnamon

Berries, for garnish (optional)

1. In a high-speed blender, add the dates, lemon juice, and salt. Carefully pour in the hot water and let soak for about 15 minutes.

2. In a large bowl, whisk the eggs until slightly frothy, about 1 minute. Add the banana, milk, oil, and vanilla and whisk until combined and mostly smooth.

3. Sift the almond flour, coconut flour, baking powder, salt, and cinnamon over the wet mixture. Whisk together until a loose batter is formed. Use the batter right away, as it will thicken if it sits. If the batter gets lumpy and doesn't flow evenly off the whisk, add 1 tablespoon of milk at a time until you reach the original consistency of the batter.

4. In a large nonstick skillet, add enough oil to just coat the bottom of the skillet, and place over medium heat. Swirl the pan to evenly distribute the oil, heating until just shimmering. Use a ladle or ¼-cup measure to spoon the batter onto the hot skillet.

5. Cook in batches until the edges are set, the bottom is golden brown, and there are a few bubbles in the pancake, 2 to 3 minutes. Since these are not traditional pancakes, you will not see as many bubbles as in a typical pancake. If you can't lift the side of the pancake with an offset spatula, wait another 30 seconds before trying again. Flip the pancake and cook until golden brown and cooked through, 1 to 2 minutes. Place the cooked pancakes on a plate covered with a clean kitchen towel to keep warm while you cook

RECIPE CONTINUES

the rest. Add more oil to the pan and repeat the process. If the pan gets too hot, remove it from the heat and let it cool before continuing.

6. Blend the dates on high until totally smooth, 45 to 60 seconds. Add more water as needed. The syrup will be quite thin when warm but will thicken up when cooled.

7. Place 2 or 3 pancakes on individual plates with date syrup and the berries (if using). Store any leftover date syrup in a covered jar in the refrigerator for up to 2 weeks. If the syrup has been in the fridge and is too thick, stir in hot water 1 tablespoon at a time until you reach your desired consistency.

NUTRITION, per 3 pancakes

| Calories: 471 | Carbs: 20 grams | Fiber: 7 grams |
| Fat: 39 grams | Protein: 16 grams | Sugar: 7 grams |

NUTRITION, per 2 tablespoons date syrup

| Calories: 103 | Carbs: 28 grams | Fiber: 3 grams |
| Fat: 0 grams | Protein: 1 gram | Sugar: 23 grams |

personal portobello shakshuka

FOR 4 SERVINGS

Shakshuka is a delicious, traditional Middle Eastern breakfast dish made up of baked eggs and a flavorful tomato sauce called matbucha. This is a super quick version of the dish, and you can make it even easier by adding the powdered spice mix to your favorite low-sugar jarred marinara sauce rather than making the sauce from scratch.

MATBUCHA TOMATO SAUCE

1 tablespoon extra-virgin olive oil

1 small shallot, finely diced (about ¼ cup)

1 garlic clove, minced (about 1 teaspoon)

½ red bell pepper, seeded, ribs removed, and diced (about ½ cup)

2 teaspoons kosher salt, plus more to taste

1 teaspoon freshly ground black pepper, plus more to taste

1 teaspoon cumin

1 teaspoon sweet paprika

1 teaspoon mild chili powder

¼ teaspoon crushed red pepper flakes (optional)

1 (15-ounce) can crushed tomatoes

SHAKSHUKA

4 large portobello caps, about 1 pound

4 large free-range eggs

¼ cup roughly chopped flat-leaf parsley, for garnish

1. Preheat the oven to 325°F.

2. In a medium saucepan, heat the oil over medium heat. Add the shallot and garlic and cook, stirring constantly, until soft, 2 to 3 minutes. Add the bell pepper and cook, stirring frequently, until soft, 2 to 3 minutes.

3. Add the salt, black pepper, cumin, paprika, chili powder, and red pepper flakes (if using). Cook until fragrant, stirring constantly, about 1 minute. Pour in the crushed tomatoes and stir to combine. Bring the mixture to a simmer and then turn the heat down to medium-low to maintain a low simmer. Continue to cook the sauce until it reduces down and becomes thick, stirring occasionally, about 12 minutes.

4. Wipe the portobellos with a clean, wet kitchen towel to remove any dirt. Using a cutlery spoon, gently scoop out the gills on the underside of the mushrooms and compost or discard.

5. Place the portobellos, with the bottom of the mushrooms facing up, on a baking sheet lined with a reusable baking mat or parchment paper. Spoon a heaping ¼ cup of the tomato sauce into each mushroom. Break an egg into a small clean bowl and then carefully pour the egg into the center of one mushroom. Continue this process with the remaining eggs. Season with salt and black pepper.

6. Bake for about 16 minutes for set whites and a runny yolk, 18 minutes for a medium egg, and 20 minutes for a completely set yolk.

7. Top with the parsley and serve immediately.

NUTRITION, per serving

| Calories: 191 | Carbs: 18 grams | Fiber: 6 grams |
| Fat: 9 grams | Protein: 13 grams | Sugar: 9 grams |

tomato toast with garlicky spinach and 2-minute poached eggs

IF MADE WITHOUT EGGS **V**

IF MADE WITH EGGS **VG**

FOR 2 SERVINGS

Poaching eggs doesn't need to cause anxiety. Don't worry, we've got you! You don't need your egg to be picture-perfect each time (reminder: nothing needs to be perfect all the time), although the vinegar and whirlpool methods in this recipe help. Packed with vitamin C, vitamin K, folic acid, iron, and calcium, spinach is one of the most nutritious vegetables you can eat, and this toast comes together as a wholesome mouth-watering breakfast.

Kosher salt

Distilled white vinegar (optional)

2 large free-range eggs

2 (1-inch-thick) slices whole-wheat sourdough bread

1 garlic clove, peeled and halved

1 medium vine-ripe tomato, halved

1 tablespoon extra-virgin olive oil

3 cups lightly packed baby spinach

Freshly ground black pepper

Crushed red pepper flakes, for garnish (optional)

1. Fill a small saucepan three-quarters full with water and bring to a strong simmer over medium heat. Season with a generous pinch of salt and stir in a splash of vinegar (if using—the vinegar helps the eggs hold together while cooking but is not essential). Break 1 egg into a ramekin and set aside.

2. Toast the bread until lightly browned and crispy. While still warm, rub the cut side of the garlic clove all over one side of each slice. Take the cut sides of the tomato and do the same, rubbing all of the juice and flesh into the bread. Set the bread aside, then mince the garlic and roughly chop the tomatoes (about 1 cup) for the next step.

3. In a sauté pan, heat the olive oil over medium until shimmering. Add the garlic and cook, stirring constantly, until soft, about 30 seconds. Add the spinach, season with salt and pepper, and cook, stirring frequently, until the spinach is just wilted, about 2 minutes.

4. Add the tomatoes to the pan with the spinach and cook, stirring frequently, until heated through, 1 to 2 minutes. Season with salt and black pepper and remove from the heat.

5. Create a whirlpool in the center of the simmering water with a slotted spoon. Once the whirlpool starts to slow down, gently drop the egg into the middle. Cook for about 2 minutes for a runny yolk, or longer if you prefer.

6. Meanwhile, place half the spinach mixture on each piece of seasoned toast.

7. Using a slotted spoon, remove the egg from the pot and dab it on a kitchen towel to remove any excess water. Place the poached egg on top of the toast and repeat the process with the other egg.

8. Sprinkle the eggs lightly with salt, then garnish with red pepper flakes (if using) and serve immediately.

NUTRITION, per serving

Calories: 343	Carbs: 41 grams	Fiber: 4 grams
Fat: 14 grams	Protein: 16 grams	Sugar: 6 grams

matcha avocado muffins

VG

MAKES 12 MUFFINS

You're going to love these muffins so matcha! A tea that is rich in antioxidants, matcha has become an increasingly popular flavor in the United States. The creamy avocado in this recipe adds healthy fats and a moist texture to these tasty green muffins—and with their dose of caffeine, they'll give you a mini boost on busy mornings.

Nonstick cooking spray

1¾ cups white whole-wheat flour

1 teaspoon baking powder

1 teaspoon baking soda

½ teaspoon kosher salt

1 tablespoon matcha powder

1 ripe avocado, pitted and peeled (about ½ cup smashed)

¾ cup organic cane sugar

2 large free-range eggs, room temperature

½ cup plain full-fat Greek yogurt, room temperature, about 4½ ounces

1½ teaspoons pure vanilla extract

¼ cup whole milk, room temperature

1. Preheat the oven to 425°F. Generously grease a muffin tin with nonstick cooking spray.

2. In a medium bowl, whisk together the flour, baking powder, baking soda, salt, and matcha. Set aside.

3. In a large bowl, use a handheld mixer to beat the avocado on medium-high until smooth and doubled in volume, 1 to 2 minutes. Add the sugar and beat on high until light, fluffy, and creamy, about 3 minutes more.

4. Add the eggs, yogurt, and vanilla to the creamed avocado. Beat on medium-high until evenly combined and creamy, scraping down the bowl as needed, about 2 minutes.

5. With the mixer off, pour the dry ingredients into the wet ingredients and beat on low until just combined. Add the milk and mix again until just combined. Pour the batter into the prepared muffin tin until about three-quarters full (a heaping ¼ cup or 2.4 ounces).

6. Bake for 5 minutes, then reduce the oven temperature to 350°F without removing the muffin tin. Bake until a toothpick inserted in the center of a muffin comes out clean and the tops are just turning golden brown, 10 to 15 minutes more. Let cool completely, then run a butter knife or offset spatula around the edges of each muffin to pop them out.

NUTRITION, per muffin

Calories: 170	Carbs: 30 grams	Fiber: 3 grams
Fat: 4 grams	Protein: 5 grams	Sugar: 15 grams

low-carb prosciutto breakfast wrap

FOR 1 SERVING

Don't assume this is any old basic wrap! This one is unique because it's the eggs that hold the wrap together—no additional wrap necessary. The salty prosciutto complements the sweet cherry tomatoes and fluffy eggs. The savory Parmesan brings all the flavors together into a mouthwatering umami bomb.

2 large free-range eggs, or 3 egg whites

Kosher salt

⅓ cup shredded Parmesan cheese

½ tablespoon unsalted grass-fed butter

2 slices prosciutto

3 large basil leaves

3 cherry tomatoes, halved

1. In a medium bowl, whisk together the eggs, salt, and 1 tablespoon of the Parmesan until well combined.

2. In a large nonstick or well-seasoned cast-iron skillet set between medium and medium-high heat, melt the butter. Pour the egg mixture into the pan, tilting it as needed so that the egg mixture reaches the edges of the pan.

3. Let the eggs cook just until they start to set, about 1 minute, then layer the prosciutto, basil, tomatoes, and remaining Parmesan on the center of the omelet.

4. Cover with a lid and cook until the eggs are fully cooked through and the cheese is mostly melted, about 2 minutes more.

5. Transfer the omelet to a plate and allow to cool enough to handle. Fold the left and right sides of the omelet and roll it from the bottom to the top to form a burrito shape. Serve immediately.

NUTRITION

Calories: 378	Carbs: 7 grams	Fiber: 1 gram
Fat: 26 grams	Protein: 29 grams	Sugar: 2 grams

spaghetti squash and kale nests

Yes, we know that kale is one of the trendiest greens around, but that's not without reason! Kale has an endless list of health benefits, but you may not know that it contains lutein, a nutrient that can protect your eyesight. Plus, spaghetti squash is high in vitamin C, which keeps your skin glowing. This breakfast dish has it all. Nutritious ingredients? Check. Fresh? Check. Yummy? Of course!

1 medium spaghetti squash, about 3 pounds

2 tablespoons avocado oil or cooking oil of choice

2 cups packed chiffonade lacinato or dinosaur kale leaves, from about 4 stalks

2 teaspoons kosher salt, plus more to taste

½ teaspoon freshly ground black pepper, plus more to taste

¾ cup shredded cheese, such as Emmental or low-sodium Monterey Jack

½ teaspoon onion powder

½ teaspoon garlic powder

¼ teaspoon crushed red pepper flakes

6 large free-range eggs

Freshly chopped parsley, for garnish

1. Place a clean, dry kitchen towel on your work surface in a nest shape and nestle the spaghetti squash on top to prevent the squash from moving around. Using a sharp knife, with the blade facing away from you, carefully poke 1-inch-wide and -deep holes lengthwise around the squash. Start from the top of the squash and move down to the bottom, then turn the squash over 180 degrees and make holes all the way around the other side, creating a dotted line lengthwise around the entire squash. This will make cutting the squash easier later and will also allow steam to escape.

2. Rub 1 tablespoon of the oil all over the squash, place it in a microwave-safe dish, and microwave on high for 8 minutes. Leave it in the microwave for 5 minutes, without opening the door, to allow the heat to finish penetrating the squash and to make it easier to handle.

3. Preheat the oven to 400°F. Line a baking sheet with a reusable baking mat or parchment paper.

4. Remove the squash from the microwave with a clean kitchen towel and carefully cut the squash in half along the perforations you made earlier. The squash should be tender and easily cut with a knife. If there is resistance, place the squash back in the microwave and microwave on high for 1 minute more. When cool enough to handle again, cut the squash in half. Gently remove the seeds and fibrous threads around the seeds, and compost or discard.

5. Using a fork, gently fluff and separate the strands of the squash, removing them from the skin, and place in a large bowl. Add the kale to the bowl.

RECIPE CONTINUES

6. Season the vegetables with salt and black pepper. Add the remaining 1 tablespoon oil, ½ cup of the cheese, the onion powder, garlic powder, and red pepper flakes and stir to combine.

7. Place the squash mixture on the baking sheet in 6 piles, about ¾ cup per pile. Shape the piles into free-form nests, pressing the middle section flat on the tray and pinching the edges together between your thumb and index finger to create a higher side that holds together. Sprinkle the remaining cheese over the nests, about 2 teaspoons per nest.

8. Bake until the edges start to brown and crisp, about 10 minutes.

9. Remove the baking sheet from the oven. Break an egg into a small clean bowl and then gently pour the egg into the center of a nest. Repeat with the remaining eggs. Season the eggs with salt and black pepper and return the nests to the oven. Continue baking for about 10 minutes for set whites and a runny yolk or about 12 minutes for a hard yolk.

10. Garnish with parsley and serve immediately.

NUTRITION, per serving

| Calories: 347 | Carbs: 23 grams | Fiber: 5 grams |
| Fat: 22 grams | Protein: 17 grams | Sugar: 9 grams |

gluten-free cauliflower bread

MAKES 1 LOAF; FOR 10 SERVINGS

This beautiful cauliflower loaf will fulfill your carb cravings without the gluten— and with a hearty dose of veggies. Perfect to enjoy with a meal (think soups and bruschetta), or by itself when you need a satisfying snack.

Nonstick cooking spray

1 large head cauliflower, about 2½ pounds, cut into florets (about 7 cups)

6 large free-range eggs

1½ cups almond flour

¼ cup grated Parmesan cheese (optional)

5 garlic cloves, minced

1 tablespoon baking powder

5 tablespoons unsalted grass-fed butter, melted and slightly cooled

½ teaspoon kosher salt

1 teaspoon Italian seasoning

1 tablespoon white sesame seeds

1 tablespoon freshly chopped parsley

1 teaspoon fresh rosemary leaves, for garnish

1. Preheat the oven to 350°F. Grease a 9 × 5-inch loaf pan with nonstick spray.

2. In a food processor, pulse the cauliflower until it reaches a rice-like consistency. You should have 3 to 4 cups.

3. Transfer the riced cauliflower to a large microwave-safe bowl and microwave it on high for about 4 minutes to steam the cauliflower and release its liquid. Set aside until cool enough to handle.

4. Transfer the riced cauliflower to a large bowl lined with cheesecloth or a kitchen towel. Tightly wrap the cauliflower and squeeze out all of the liquid until the cauliflower is dry and crumbles between your fingers. Set aside the cauliflower.

5. Separate the eggs, placing the yolks and whites into two separate large bowls. Beat the whites with a handheld mixer until stiff peaks form.

6. Add about one-quarter of the beaten whites to the yolks. Add the almond flour, Parmesan (if using), garlic, baking powder, butter, and salt. Gently mix with a rubber spatula until combined.

7. Add the remaining egg whites, the riced cauliflower, and Italian seasoning. Gently fold the ingredients together until just combined. Do not overmix, as this will break down the egg whites.

8. Transfer the mixture to the prepared loaf pan and sprinkle the top with the sesame seeds, parsley, and rosemary.

9. Bake until the bread is golden brown on top and a wooden skewer inserted into the center of the bread comes out clean, 45 to 50 minutes.

10. Let cool before cutting the loaf into 10 slices and serving as desired. Refrigerate any leftovers, wrapped in a reusable beeswax wrap or in an airtight container, for up to 5 days.

NUTRITION, per slice

| Calories: 239 | Carbs: 10 grams | Fiber: 5 grams |
| Fat: 19 grams | Protein: 11 grams | Sugar: 3 grams |

prep

"

Being prepared is a great way to remove unnecessary stress from your life.

"

prepare for the best

Meal-prep is a great way to start your busy week on the right foot. This chapter shares quick recipes that will last in the fridge throughout the week. We included different treatments and variations with each so you don't get bored eating the same dish every day. You can also pop each dish in the freezer to save for a rainy day or for a week when you don't have time to meal prep. Just make sure to label and date the containers, because you WILL forget what's in them—trust us on this.

roasted cauliflower and curry soup

MAKES ABOUT 8½ CUPS; FOR 4 SERVINGS

This fragrant vegan and gluten-free soup has a deep and earthy flavor from the curry seasoning and pepitas (pumpkin seeds). These tiny seeds pack a big nutritional punch, as they are rich in magnesium. The velvety coconut milk in this recipe adds a silky creaminess that you'll crave again and again. You can store this soup in the fridge for a delicious meal-prepped lunch or freeze it for up to three months. Win!

SPICED PEPITAS

½ cup raw pepitas (pumpkin seeds)

1 teaspoon unrefined coconut oil, melted

½ teaspoon curry powder

¼ teaspoon garlic powder

¼ teaspoon onion powder

¼ teaspoon kosher salt

SOUP

1 medium head cauliflower, about 2¼ pounds, cut into florets (about 6 cups)

3 tablespoons unrefined coconut oil, melted

Kosher salt and freshly ground black pepper

1 small yellow onion, about 8 ounces, diced (about 1½ cups)

1 jalapeño, about 1 ounce, seeded if desired, diced (about ¼ cup)

2 garlic cloves, minced

3 tablespoons red curry paste

1 (14-ounce) can unsweetened coconut milk, about 1¾ cups

4 cups vegetable broth

Sliced scallions, for serving

Fresh cilantro, for serving

Lime wedges, for serving

1. Preheat the oven to 375°F.

2. Combine the pepitas, melted coconut oil, curry powder, garlic powder, onion powder, and salt on a small baking sheet lined with a reusable baking mat or parchment paper. Stir until the pepitas are completely coated in the spices, then spread out in an even layer.

3. Bake until the pepitas start to puff up (you might even hear them pop!) and are lightly toasted, about 8 minutes, stirring once halfway through. Set aside to cool completely.

4. Increase the oven temperature to 450°F.

5. Arrange the cauliflower on another baking sheet lined with a reusable baking mat or parchment paper. Drizzle with 1 tablespoon of the melted coconut oil and season with salt and pepper. Toss to coat, then spread out in an even layer.

6. Roast until tender and browned in spots, about 20 minutes, flipping the cauliflower once halfway through.

7. Heat the remaining 2 tablespoons coconut oil in a large saucepan over medium-high heat. Add the onion and jalapeño, and cook until the onion begins to caramelize, about 5 minutes.

8. Add the garlic and continue to cook until the garlic is toasted and fragrant, about 2 minutes more. Add the curry paste and cook, stirring to dissolve, for about 1 minute.

9. Stir in the coconut milk and vegetable broth and season with salt and pepper. Remove from the heat.

10. Combine the roasted cauliflower and the broth in a blender, or use an immersion blender to purée the soup directly in the pot. If your blender is not big enough to blend all the soup at once, blend the soup in 2 batches. Remove the small cap from the lid of the blender, then cover the opening with a kitchen towel (this will help to release excess steam while blending). Purée until smooth. Season with salt and pepper, if needed.

11. Allow the soup to cool completely before ladling into containers with locking lids or mason jars. Keep the crispy pepitas in a separate airtight container (a dressing container would be perfect) for up to 4 months in a cool, dry place. The soup will keep for up to 5 days in the refrigerator or for up to 3 months in the freezer. Serve cold or heat in the microwave on high for 3 minutes, stirring halfway through.

12. To serve, top with the crispy pepitas, scallions, and cilantro, and serve with lime wedges.

NUTRITION, per serving of soup and
2 tablespoons of pepitas

| Calories: 395 | Carbs: 31 grams | Fiber: 10 grams |
| Fat: 29 grams | Protein: 11 grams | Sugar: 10 grams |

broiled chicken shawarma
with garlicky white sauce

FOR 5 SERVINGS

Shawarma is a delectable, succulent meat dish served throughout the Middle East and is typically prepared on a rotating rotisserie. There are many variations of shawarma, so there's no wrong way to make it! This at-home version doesn't include the traditional spit-roast, but it *does* have all of the aromatic spices and flavors. You can quadruple the spice blend used here and store it in an airtight container for up to six months.

SHAWARMA MARINADE

1 teaspoon cumin

1 teaspoon ground cardamom

1 tablespoon paprika

½ teaspoon cinnamon

1 teaspoon ground turmeric

1 teaspoon garlic powder

1 tablespoon ground sumac

¼ teaspoon cayenne pepper

1 tablespoon kosher salt

1 teaspoon freshly ground black pepper

¼ cup extra-virgin olive oil

1 tablespoon freshly squeezed lemon juice

3 garlic cloves, sliced

2 pounds boneless, skinless, chicken thighs, trimmed

GARLICKY YOGURT SAUCE

1 cup plain whole-milk Greek yogurt, about 8 ounces

1 tablespoon freshly squeezed lemon juice

1 garlic clove, grated

1 teaspoon sumac

⅛ teaspoon cayenne pepper

¼ teaspoon kosher salt

¼ teaspoon freshly ground black pepper

1. In a large bowl, combine all the marinade ingredients and whisk together. Add the chicken thighs and coat evenly. Cover and chill for at least 1 hour or up to overnight.

2. In a small bowl, stir together all the sauce ingredients. Season with additional salt if needed. Cover and refrigerate until ready to use. (You can do this the night before so the ingredients get to know one another and marinate.)

3. When you're ready to cook, position an oven rack about 6 inches from the broiler source, then preheat the broiler. Line a baking sheet with a reusable baking mat or foil, and fit a wire rack into the baking sheet.

4. Place the chicken in a single layer on the prepared wire rack, smooth-sides down. Pick off any garlic on top of the chicken (it might burn while the chicken cooks). Broil until the chicken is well browned and registers at least 165°F, 16 to 20 minutes. You may need to rotate the pan halfway through if your broiler heats unevenly. Remove and let the chicken rest.

5. Slice the chicken into strips and let cool completely before packing into individual reusable containers.

NUTRITION, per serving of chicken and 2 tablespoons of sauce

| Calories: 565 | Carbs: 29 grams | Fiber: 3 grams |
| Fat: 27 grams | Protein: 54 grams | Sugar: 3 grams |

MEAL-PREP TWISTS

DAY 1: Serve with a salad of chopped romaine, cucumbers, and cherry tomatoes. Thin the yogurt sauce with a few tablespoons of water for the dressing.

DAY 2: Stuff in a warm whole-wheat pita with sliced cucumbers, tomatoes, pickles, and prepared yogurt sauce.

DAY 3: Spoon over brown rice or whole-wheat couscous with fresh parsley and yogurt sauce.

DAY 4: Warm in homemade or store-bought chicken bone broth with chickpeas, diced tomatoes, and scallions. Top with yogurt sauce before serving.

TIP

Turn plain nondairy yogurt into Greek yogurt by straining it through cheesecloth.

freezer-prep mushroom and chicken burritos

MAKES 6 BURRITOS

This recipe includes both veggie and chicken options, so feel free to double up on your favorite filling. The mushroom version is loaded with tons of vitamins for heart health and is a great choice for vegetarians (they can also be made vegan with dairy-free cheese). The chicken version has a bit more protein, but both are incredibly delicious!

SPICED MUSHROOM FILLING (MAKES ABOUT 3 CUPS)

1 tablespoon avocado oil or cooking oil of choice

½ yellow onion, thinly sliced (about 1 heaping cup)

1½ pounds mixed mushrooms, such as cremini, shiitake, and king oyster, cleaned and diced (about 8 cups)

1 teaspoon kosher salt

½ teaspoon freshly ground black pepper

1 teaspoon cumin

1 teaspoon chili powder

½ teaspoon garlic powder

CHICKEN FILLING (MAKES ABOUT 3 CUPS)

1 tablespoon avocado oil or cooking oil of choice

½ yellow onion, thinly sliced (about 1 heaping cup)

2 boneless, skinless chicken breasts, thinly sliced

½ teaspoon kosher salt

¼ teaspoon freshly ground black pepper

½ cup jarred salsa

TO ASSEMBLE

⅓ cup finely chopped cilantro

Juice of 1 lime (about 2 tablespoons)

1½ cups cooked brown rice, about 9 ounces

6 (10-inch) multigrain low-carb tortillas

1 (16-ounce) can low-sodium refried black beans, prepared according to package directions and cooled

1½ cups low-sodium Mexican-blend shredded cheese

1. Heat a large skillet over medium-high. Add the oil and onion and cook, stirring constantly, until the onion starts to soften, 2 to 3 minutes.

2. Push the onion to one side of the skillet and add the mushrooms in one even layer. Allow the mushrooms to cook, undisturbed, until a crust forms on the bottom, 10 to 12 minutes. The mushrooms will slump and release a lot of moisture, but once the liquid evaporates, the mushrooms will get nice and brown. After the mushrooms have formed a crust on one side, stir the onion into the mushrooms, scraping up any browned bits at the bottom of the pan. Cook, stirring occasionally, until the mushrooms and onion are well browned, about 5 minutes.

3. Reduce the heat to medium and add the salt, pepper, cumin, chili powder, and garlic powder. Cook, stirring until fragrant, about 2 minutes. Remove from the skillet and set aside to cool.

4. Place the skillet back on the stove (there's no need to wipe it clean) over medium-high heat. Add the oil and onion and cook, stirring constantly, until the onion starts to soften, 2 to 3 minutes.

5. Push the onion to one side, add the chicken, and season with the salt and pepper. Cook, undisturbed, until a brown crust begins to form, 2 to 3 minutes. Flip the chicken. Reduce the heat to medium and add the salsa, scraping up any browned bits from the skillet, and stir to coat the chicken. Cook until the chicken is cooked through, about 4 minutes more. Remove from the skillet and set aside to cool.

6. Stir the cilantro and lime juice into the rice.

7. Assemble the burritos by microwaving each tortilla for about 15 seconds, or warm them individually in the skillet, about 15 seconds on each side. Layer each tortilla, starting with a scant ⅓ cup of the refried beans, then ¼ cup of the flavored rice. Top half of the tortillas with about 1 cup each of the mushroom filling and half with about 1 cup each of the chicken, and top each with ¼ cup of the cheese.

8. Fold in the left and right sides of the tortilla and roll it up from the bottom, tucking the bottom edge under the filling. Wrap in parchment paper or reusable beeswax wrap and label. Place the burritos in a reusable zip-top bag or freezer container. Freeze for up to 3 months.

9. To reheat after being frozen, remove a burrito from the parchment paper, wrap it in a damp paper towel, and microwave on high until the center is hot, 2 to 3 minutes, flipping halfway through. Let stand for 1 minute before serving.

NUTRITION, per 1 mushroom burrito (with cheese)

Calories: 579	Carbs: 87 grams	Fiber: 16 grams
Fat: 17 grams	Protein: 24 grams	Sugar: 8 grams

NUTRITION, per 1 chicken burrito

Calories: 694	Carbs: 73 grams	Fiber: 11 grams
Fat: 20 grams	Protein: 54 grams	Sugar: 3 grams

honey-mustard chicken
with roasted garden veggies

FOR 4 SERVINGS

Warning: The tangy-sweet honey mustard glaze here is addictive. This quick-and-easy meal-prep recipe has it all—starch, protein, and vegetables—plus, it's totally versatile, so you won't tire of it. Whether you prepare this dish as a salad, sandwich, or bowl, we know you'll love it.

1 medium sweet potato, diced
(about 3 cups)

1 cup diced red potatoes, about 6 ounces

1 small red onion, diced (about 1½ cups)

1 cup quartered Brussels sprouts

1 cup chopped green beans, about 4 ounces

1 cup chopped carrot

Extra-virgin olive oil

Kosher salt and freshly ground black pepper

1½ teaspoons freshly chopped thyme

1 tablespoon fresh rosemary leaves

¼ cup Dijon mustard

¼ cup raw honey

3 garlic cloves, minced

2 pounds bone-in, skin-on chicken thighs

1. Preheat the oven to 400°F and line a baking sheet with a reusable baking mat or parchment paper.

2. Place the sweet potato, red potatoes, red onion, Brussels sprouts, green beans, and carrot on the baking sheet in separate piles.

3. Drizzle with olive oil and sprinkle with salt, pepper, the thyme, and the rosemary. Maintaining the separate piles, toss to coat, then spread into one even layer. Set aside.

4. In a small bowl, combine the mustard, honey, garlic, and ¼ teaspoon each of salt and pepper. Whisk until smooth. Set aside.

5. Coat a large cast-iron skillet with olive oil and place the chicken thighs skin-side down in the pan. Season with salt and pepper, then spoon over or brush generously with half of the honey-mustard sauce. Flip the chicken thighs, season with salt and pepper, then brush with the remaining honey-mustard sauce.

6. Place the vegetables and the chicken in the oven on separate racks. Bake until the chicken reaches an internal temperature of 165°F and the potatoes are tender, about 30 minutes. (Optional: Remove the vegetables once cooked and broil the chicken until the skin crisps up, 1 to 2 minutes.)

7. Set aside to cool. Distribute into four individual resealable containers, mixing up the combination of vegetables so that you get something a little different each day.

8. Cover and store in the refrigerator for up to 4 days.

NUTRITION, per serving

| Calories: 627 | Carbs: 55 grams | Fiber: 7 grams |
| Fat: 28 grams | Protein: 45 grams | Sugar: 28 grams |

MEAL-PREP TWISTS

1. Shred some chicken and add to a mason jar. Layer with vegetables and top with sliced romaine for an on-the-go salad.

2. Dice some chicken. Add the chicken and some veggies to homemade whole-wheat croutons for a quick honey-mustard panzanella salad.

3. Toast a slice of sprouted grain bread. Top with mashed avocado and add chicken and vegetables for an open-faced sandwich.

4. Add chicken and veggies to whole-wheat couscous with sliced almonds.

teriyaki edamame turkey meatballs

MAKES 25 MEATBALLS; FOR 5 SERVINGS

This Asian-inspired twist on a classic dish is an enticing choice for this week's meal prep. The edamame in these meatballs adds extra protein, a nice textural element, and fun pop of color. Also, our sweet teriyaki sauce is a beautiful blend of robust ingredients, including ginger, which is great for digestion and adds a little kick too.

MEATBALLS

¾ cup frozen shelled edamame, thawed

2 scallions, roughly chopped (about ¼ cup)

2 garlic cloves, roughly chopped (about 2 teaspoons)

½ inch fresh ginger, peeled and grated

1¾ teaspoons kosher salt

½ teaspoon freshly ground black pepper

1 pound 93% lean ground turkey

½ cup crispy brown rice cereal, or panko if gluten isn't a concern

1 large free-range egg

2 heaping cups snow peas, about 6 ounces

LOW-SUGAR TERIYAKI SAUCE

¾ cup low-sodium tamari

¼ cup rice wine vinegar

2 tablespoons raw honey

2 garlic cloves, grated (about 1½ teaspoons)

1 inch fresh ginger, peeled and grated (about 2 teaspoons)

3 scallions, thinly sliced (about ⅓ cup)

1½ teaspoons cornstarch

2 tablespoons water

TO SERVE

1 tablespoon toasted sesame seeds

2 tablespoons thinly sliced scallions

1 carrot, julienned or thinly sliced

1. Preheat the oven to 375°F. Line two baking sheets with reusable baking mats or parchment paper.

2. In a food processor, place the edamame, scallions, garlic, ginger, salt, and pepper. Pulse about 25 times, scraping down the sides of the bowl as needed, until evenly incorporated without any large chunks of vegetables. Add the turkey, cereal, and egg. Pulse until the mixture is evenly combined, another 15 to 20 times, scraping down the sides of the bowl halfway through.

3. Using a 1-ounce scoop or well-rounded tablespoon, portion out the meatball mixture. Roll a scoop of the mixture between your hands to shape it into a ball. Place on one of the prepared baking sheets. If the meat mixture is too sticky, place it in the fridge until firm, about 20 minutes, and then form the meatballs.

4. Bake until brown and crispy on the top and bottom and cooked through, 20 to 25 minutes.

5. Spread the snow peas evenly on the remaining baking sheet and bake for the meatballs' last 5 minutes in the oven. The snow peas are done when they turn a bright green and just begin to soften but still have a crunch. Remove the peas and the meatballs from the oven and let cool.

6. Heat a small saucepan over medium. Combine the tamari, vinegar, honey, garlic, ginger, and scallions in the pan and bring to a simmer. Cook until the scallions become tender, 2 to 3 minutes.

7. In a small bowl, mix the cornstarch and water to make a slurry. While whisking, pour the slurry into the simmering teriyaki sauce. Whisking constantly, simmer until the sauce is thickened and the whisk leaves a trail behind it through the sauce, about 2 minutes. Remove from the heat and set aside.

8. Divide the meatballs and snow peas among five individual airtight containers. Divide the sauce evenly over the meatballs. Allow the meatballs and the sauce to cool completely before storing. Label and date, then store in the freezer for up to 6 months. Serve with sesame seeds, sliced scallions, and julienned carrot.

NUTRITION, per serving

| Calories: 378 | Carbs: 20 grams | Fiber: 4 grams |
| Fat: 19 grams | Protein: 33 grams | Sugar: 10 grams |

MEAL-PREP TWISTS

1. Serve with steamed brown rice.

2. Fill a few pieces of green-leaf lettuce to make lettuce wraps.

3. Reheat in store-bought or homemade chicken bone broth.

4. Add to chilled, cooked buckwheat noodles.

buffalo chickpea grain bowls

(v)

FOR 5 SERVINGS

This vegan take on Buffalo sauce is the perfect combination of zest and heat (without being too spicy!). Mixed with chickpeas, this dish is an excellent choice for when you're being mindful of your meat intake. Farro is a wonderful grain with a nutty flavor and chewy texture. It's loaded with protein, iron, and magnesium, which will keep you energized all day.

GRAINS

3 cups low-sodium vegetable stock

1 teaspoon kosher salt

1½ cups uncooked farro, about 9½ ounces

BUFFALO SAUCE

2 tablespoons avocado oil or cooking oil of choice

1 medium yellow onion, about 7½ ounces, grated (about 1 cup)

2 garlic cloves minced

1 carrot, grated (about ½ cup)

Kosher salt

¼ teaspoon cayenne pepper (optional)

2 teaspoons paprika

1 teaspoon cumin

1 tablespoon tomato paste

½ cup low-sodium vegetable stock

2 tablespoons cider vinegar

1 tablespoon coconut sugar

½ cup low-sodium hot sauce (look for mild if you are heat sensitive)

2 (15-ounce) cans no-salt-added chickpeas, drained and rinsed

SUGGESTED TOPPINGS

2 celery stalks, thinly sliced on a bias

1 carrot, julienned

5 small radishes, thinly sliced

Vegan Ranch (page 227)

1. In a medium saucepan over medium heat, bring the vegetable stock and salt to a boil. Add the farro, stir, reduce the heat to a simmer, and cover. Cook until tender, 20 to 25 minutes, or according to the package directions. If the liquid has not evaporated by the time the farro is tender, drain the farro and discard the liquid.

2. Heat the oil in a tall pan over medium. When the oil is shimmering, add the onion, garlic, and carrot, and cook, stirring frequently, until the excess liquid from the onion has evaporated and the vegetables are softened, 6 to 7 minutes. Season the vegetables with salt.

3. Add the cayenne (if using), paprika, and cumin, stirring to combine. Toast the spices until fragrant, about 2 minutes. Add the tomato paste, stirring to evenly combine all the ingredients. Toast the tomato paste until it becomes dark red and fragrant, about 2 minutes.

4. Pour in the vegetable stock and deglaze the pan. Add the vinegar, sugar, and hot sauce, stirring to combine. Bring to a low simmer over medium heat.

5. Add the chickpeas, stirring to combine, and simmer until the sauce is reduced and the chickpeas are warmed through, about 12 minutes. Season with salt.

6. Let the farro and Buffalo chickpeas cool completely before dividing into four airtight individual containers.

NOTE

If eating a grain bowl within 4 days, top with the celery, carrot, and radishes and refrigerate. Add the vegan ranch from a dressing container.

If freezing, add only the farro and chickpeas. Label and date. The farro and chickpeas will keep in the freezer for up to 6 months. When ready to eat, defrost in the refrigerator overnight, reheat, and top with fresh vegetables and dressing to serve.

NUTRITION, per serving (not including toppings)

| Calories: 484 | Carbs: 80 grams | Fiber: 18 grams |
| Fat: 11 grams | Protein: 21 grams | Sugar: 17 grams |

slow-cooker roasted tomato-basil soup

FOR 8 SERVINGS

There's nothing more comforting than a good bowl of tomato soup. This versatile soup can shapeshift into gazpacho, marinara, or even a curry sauce—check out our meal-prep twists.

2 pounds Roma or vine-ripened tomatoes (about 8 tomatoes), cored and roughly chopped into 2-inch pieces

1 red bell pepper, seeded and sliced into ½-inch strips

1 medium yellow onion, quartered

6 garlic cloves, smashed and peeled

½ cup extra-virgin olive oil

Kosher salt and freshly ground black pepper

1 teaspoon dried oregano

1 teaspoon dried thyme

1 tablespoon tomato paste

2 cups low-sodium vegetable stock

½ cup fresh basil leaves, plus more for garnish

1. Preheat the oven to 425°F.

2. Place the tomatoes on one lined baking sheet; place the peppers, onions, and garlic on another lined baking sheet. Drizzle both sheets with the olive oil and season with salt and pepper.

3. Roast, stirring halfway through, until the vegetables are browned on the edges and fragrant, about 30 minutes.

4. Transfer the roasted vegetables to a slow cooker, making sure to pour in any excess juices from the pan. Add the oregano, thyme, tomato paste, and vegetable stock.

5. Cover and cook on high for 2 hours, until the soup is slightly thickened and the tomatoes are slightly breaking down.

6. Using an immersion blender or a standing blender, purée the soup until creamy and smooth. Season with salt and pepper.

7. Stack and roll the basil leaves, then thinly slice. Add the basil to the soup and stir to incorporate. Ladle the warm soup into bowls and garnish with more basil.

NUTRITION, per serving

| Calories: 159 | Carbs: 9 grams | Fiber: 2 grams |
| Fat: 14 grams | Protein: 2 grams | Sugar: 5 grams |

MEAL-PREP TWISTS

1. Make low-carb chips to serve with the soup. Preheat the oven to 325°F. On a baking sheet lined with a reusable baking mat or parchment paper, bake ¼-cup piles of shredded Parmesan cheese until melted, just bubbling, and golden brown, 8 to 10 minutes. Allow to cool before removing from the baking sheet. Store in an airtight container.

2. Serve cold as a simple refreshing gazpacho.

3. Reduce in a saucepan until it reaches your desired thickness and use as a marinara on brown rice pasta.

4. Transform the soup into a creamy curry. Toast 1½ teaspoons curry powder in a dry, hot pan until fragrant, about 30 seconds. Add ½ cup coconut milk and 1 cup of the tomato soup. Simmer until heated to your desired temperature, about 10 minutes.

balsamic-soy salmon and veggie bake

FOR 4 SERVINGS

With this recipe you can conveniently bake your salmon and veggies together on the same baking sheet. We love this simple meal because of the fruity, tart balsamic vinegar and the salty, rich soy sauce in the marinade for the salmon. Feel free to switch out the veggies here for your favorites!

BALSAMIC SOY MARINADE

¼ cup soy sauce

¼ cup balsamic vinegar

1½ tablespoons extra-virgin olive oil

2 garlic cloves, minced

4 (6-ounce) skin-on salmon fillets

GARLIC-PAPRIKA SPICE RUB

1 teaspoon garlic powder

1 teaspoon paprika

1 teaspoon onion powder

1 teaspoon kosher salt

½ teaspoon freshly ground black pepper

VEGGIE BAKE

1 large carrot, about 4½ ounces, thinly sliced on the bias (about 1 scant cup)

5 ounces green beans, ends trimmed

5 ounces asparagus, ends trimmed, cut into 2-inch pieces (about 1 heaping cup)

1 medium yellow squash, chopped (about 1½ cups)

Extra-virgin olive oil

Kosher salt and freshly ground black pepper

1. In a 9-inch square baking dish or reusable zip-top bag, combine the soy sauce, balsamic vinegar, oil, and garlic and whisk to combine.

2. Put two of the salmon fillets in the marinade, making sure all sides are coated. Transfer to the refrigerator to marinate for at least 30 minutes or up to 2 hours.

3. Preheat the oven to 450°F. Line a baking sheet with a reusable baking mat or parchment paper.

4. In a small bowl, mix together the garlic powder, paprika, onion powder, salt, and pepper. Evenly coat the remaining salmon fillets with the spice rub.

5. Place all of the salmon and vegetables on the baking dish. Drizzle the vegetables with olive oil and season with salt and pepper. Mix to evenly coat, being careful not to mix the vegetables together.

6. Bake for about 11 minutes per inch of salmon thickness, until the flesh is firm and just opaque.

7. Allow the salmon and vegetables to cool completely before dividing them into four reusable lunch containers. Mix and match the vegetables to your liking. Refrigerate for up to 3 days.

NUTRITION, per serving

Calories: 500	Carbs: 15 grams	Fiber: 4 grams
Fat: 30 grams	Protein: 42 grams	Sugar: 7 grams

instant pot chipotle carnitas

DF

FOR 5 SERVINGS

Simmering tender pork in this smoky, spicy sauce makes each dish you build from this meal prep delicious and exciting. You can find cans of the chipotles in adobo sauce used in this recipe at most grocery stores. The chipotles are dried, smoked jalapeños and the adobo is a tangy, sweet red sauce. These bold flavors will heighten from the pressure cooker for a fragrant and nutritious meal.

2½ pounds pork shoulder, trimmed and cut into 1-inch chunks

2 tablespoons kosher salt, plus more to taste

1 tablespoon freshly ground black pepper, plus more to taste

1 tablespoon avocado oil or cooking oil of choice

2 medium yellow onions, about 1 pound 3 ounces, peeled and quartered

1 carrot, cut into 1-inch pieces

1 garlic head, cut in half horizontally

1 (7-ounce) can chipotles in adobo sauce (if you are spice-averse, use half the can, or use just the sauce and save the peppers for another use or compost them)

1 orange, peeled and cut into eighths

1 tablespoon cumin

1½ teaspoons ground coriander

3 bay leaves

1. Heat a 6-quart electric pressure cooker to sear by choosing the "more sauté" option. In a large bowl, season the pork on all sides with the salt and pepper. Add the oil to the hot pot. When the oil is shimmering, sear the pork in batches until browned on all sides, 8 to 10 minutes per batch, turning as needed.

2. Return all the pork to the pressure cooker, along with the onions, carrot, garlic, chipotles, orange wedges, cumin, coriander, and bay leaves. Cover the ingredients a third of the way with water, 2 to 2½ cups.

3. Secure the lid on the pressure cooker, ensuring the top pressure nozzle is pointing toward "sealing." Pressure cook on high for 40 minutes. Allow the pressure cooker to slowly release pressure for 25 to 30 minutes before turning the pressure nozzle to "venting." (Quick release will toughen the meat, as the quick change in pressure could cause the meat to seize up.)

4. Transfer the pork to a platter. Strain the cooking liquid back into the electric pressure cooker and set to "more sauté." Bring to a boil and reduce by half, to about 2½ cups, 20 to 25 minutes. Compost or discard the vegetables and solids. When the sauce is reduced, taste and add salt and pepper, if necessary.

5. Shred the pork with two forks, season with salt and pepper, and add it back to the cooking liquid.

6. Allow the carnitas to cool before dividing it among five individual airtight containers. This is a great make-ahead meal that freezes wonderfully for up to 6 months. Defrost overnight in the refrigerator.

NUTRITION, per serving

| Calories: 764 | Carbs: 18 grams | Fiber: 4 grams |
| Fat: 52 grams | Protein: 55 grams | Sugar: 9 grams |

MEAL-PREP TWISTS

1. Add to shredded kale, canned beans, and steamed rice for a burrito bowl.

2. Stir-fry with leftover rice and vegetables for a fun fusion pork fried rice.

3. Add to a multigrain tortilla with cheese and spinach for a quesadilla.

4. Serve with roasted vegetables.

5. Preheat the oven to 350°F. Mix 1 packed cup of the carnitas with ¼ cup black beans and ½ cup riced cauliflower. Add the mixture to 2 hollowed-out bell peppers. Top each with 1 tablespoon shredded cheese. Place on a baking sheet and wrap foil around the base of each pepper to keep it from falling over when baking. Bake until the peppers are soft and the cheese is melted, 25 to 30 minutes.

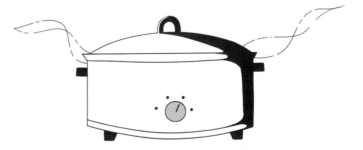

solo

"

Self-care can mean
a lot of things, but
the foundation of it
is understanding
the core things that
make you *you*.

"

flying solo

Cooking for yourself can be a beautiful form of self-care. Pour a glass of wine (or whatever your preferred beverage is), turn on your favorite show, and make it a date with yourself. These are delicious meals for when it's just you—when you're ready to relax after a long day or just spend some time on your own. Some portions are a bit bigger so you can pack the leftovers for lunch later in the week or have them for dinner the next day.

one-pan teriyaki tofu

FOR 2 SERVINGS

Heads up—tofu tastes better the longer you marinate it for, so make sure to plan at least a day ahead for this one. Though, if you're in a bind, you can cut down on the pressing and marinating time and your meal will still have plenty of flavor, so no worries! Once the tofu is marinated, the recipe really doesn't take much more time. This recipe is an incredible dish for when you're looking for a meat-free meal (or even when you're not—it's that good).

14 ounces extra-firm tofu

TERIYAKI MARINADE

½ cup low-sodium soy sauce

¼ cup raw honey

2 teaspoons sesame seeds

1 teaspoon sesame oil

1 inch fresh ginger, sliced

3 garlic cloves, minced

½ scallion, white part only, thinly sliced (about 1 tablespoon), reserve green part for garnish

VEGETABLES

1 small carrot, sliced (about ½ cup)

1 small red bell pepper, chopped (about 1 cup)

1 cup broccoli florets

Kosher salt and freshly ground black pepper

1 to 2 cups cooked brown rice or brown rice pasta, for serving

½ scallion, green part only, thinly sliced, for garnish

1. Cut the tofu into 12 pieces, keeping the block intact. Place a clean kitchen towel on a plate and place the tofu on top. Encase the tofu in the towel and put something heavy on top, such as a cast-iron skillet or a heavy can on a flat plate. Let sit for at least 30 minutes or up to overnight.

2. In a small bowl, mix the soy sauce, honey, sesame seeds, sesame oil, ginger, garlic, and scallions. Put the tofu in a medium dish and pour the marinade over the top. Cover and refrigerate for at least 1 hour. It's even better if you can do this in the morning before you leave for work.

3. Preheat the oven to 450°F.

4. Fold a large piece of parchment paper in half, then open it back up. Place the parchment on a baking sheet.

5. Place the carrot, bell pepper, and broccoli on one half of the parchment paper, close to the middle seam. Season with salt and pepper.

6. Lay the tofu on the veggies and spoon over a few tablespoons of the marinade to season the vegetables. Fold the parchment back in half, covering the tofu and veggies. Starting from the bottom, where the folded seam meets an opening, cinch the paper together by folding it over itself along the edges. Continue folding the parchment over itself until closed on all sides.

RECIPE CONTINUES

7. Bake until the tofu is completely warmed through and the vegetables are tender-crisp, about 15 minutes. Unwrap the parchment paper, being careful of the hot steam in the package.

8. Serve over rice or pasta, with a sprinkle of scallions. Save half the tofu in an airtight container for another meal later in the week.

NUTRITION, tofu, rice, and vegetables only

| Calories: 515 | Carbs: 28 grams | Fiber: 13 grams |
| Fat: 14 grams | Protein: 31 grams | Sugar: 13 grams |

NUTRITION, per ¼ cup sauce

| Calories: 64 | Carbs: 73 grams | Fiber: 1 gram |
| Fat: 3 grams | Protein: 5 grams | Sugar: 2 grams |

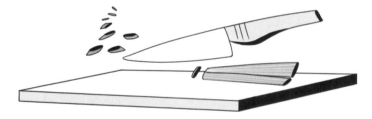

no-cook tuna avocado wrap

(DF)

FOR 1 SERVING

We had you at no-cook, didn't we? Canned tuna is a staple item in many of our pantries. It's inexpensive, easy to prepare, and an excellent source of protein and omega-3 fatty acids, which support brain function and lower cholesterol. This recipe uses avocado instead of mayo, which is a simple swap for healthy fats. Pro tip: Buy canned light or skipjack tuna instead of canned white tuna to reduce your mercury exposure, and choose wild sustainably caught brands, if possible.

1 (5-ounce) can tuna in olive oil, drained

½ large avocado, diced (about ½ cup)

1 small carrot, finely diced (about ⅓ cup)

1 celery stalk, finely diced (about ½ cup)

2 scallions, thinly sliced (about ¼ cup)

2 tablespoons chopped walnuts, toasted if desired

1 tablespoon Dijon mustard

1 tablespoon freshly squeezed lemon juice

¼ teaspoon garlic powder

Kosher salt and freshly ground black pepper

1 large or 2 small whole-wheat tortillas

2 pieces green-leaf lettuce

1. In a large bowl, add the tuna and avocado. Use a fork to gently break up the tuna and combine with avocado, leaving some chunks.

2. Add the carrot, celery, scallions, walnuts, mustard, lemon juice, garlic powder, salt, and pepper. Stir to combine. (This makes about 2 cups.)

3. Lay the tortilla flat on a plate. Layer the lettuce leaves in the center of the tortilla, then top with the tuna mixture, spreading it out as needed to cover the lettuce. Carefully roll up to create a wrap (or two).

NUTRITION

| Calories: 639 | Carbs: 43 grams | Fiber: 17 grams |
| Fat: 31 grams | Protein: 52 grams | Sugar: 7 grams |

spiced tahini loaded sweet potato

FOR 1 SERVING

Sumac is a Middle Eastern spice with a tangy lemony flavor. You may know tahini—a condiment made from toasted ground sesame—from hummus, baba ghanoush, or halva. The tahini in this recipe replaces butter and sour cream for a nutritious version of the traditional baked potato. Plus, sweet potatoes have more vitamin A and vitamin C and potassium than white potatoes.

SWEET POTATO

1 medium sweet potato

8 ounces can no-salt-added chickpeas, drained

2 teaspoons avocado oil or cooking oil of choice

1 teaspoon kosher salt

¼ teaspoon freshly ground black pepper, plus more to taste

¼ teaspoon cumin

¼ teaspoon ground sumac

**TAHINI DRESSING
(MAKES ABOUT ½ CUP)**

¼ cup tahini (about 2 ounces)

Juice of ½ lemon (about 2 tablespoons)

1 garlic clove, grated

¼ teaspoon kosher salt, plus more to taste

TOPPINGS

2 tablespoons pomegranate seeds

2 tablespoons roughly chopped flat-leaf parsley

4 mint leaves, hand-torn

1. Preheat the oven to 400°F. Line a baking sheet.

2. Cut the potato in half lengthwise and add to the baking sheet along with the chickpeas. Drizzle with oil and season with salt, rubbing to ensure even coverage.

3. Turn the potato halves flesh-side down and roast until the potatoes are tender and the chickpeas are crispy, 25 to 30 minutes, stirring the chickpeas once halfway through.

4. In a small bowl, mix together the dressing ingredients. It should be similar to the consistency of ranch dressing. Stir in 1 to 2 tablespoons of water if needed.

5. Remove the baking sheet from oven. Place the sweet potato halves flesh-side up on a plate. Sprinkle the chickpeas with the pepper, cumin, and sumac. Toss to coat. Set aside.

6. Scoop the flesh out of the potato halves into a small bowl. Mix half of the tahini dressing with the flesh of the sweet potato, then use a fork to mash the potato until smooth. Taste and add more salt and pepper if needed. Spoon the seasoned potato flesh back into the skins.

7. Top with half the spiced chickpeas, the pomegranate seeds, parsley, and mint. Drizzle with extra dressing, if desired. Save half the roasted chickpeas in an airtight container for a spicy weekday snack.

NUTRITION, sweet potato, chickpeas, and seasonings

| Calories: 630 | Carbs: 103 grams | Fiber: 23 grams |
| Fat: 16 grams | Protein: 23 grams | Sugar: 24 grams |

NUTRITION, 2 servings of tahini dressing

| Calories: 404 | Carbs: 23 grams | Fiber: 7 grams |
| Fat: 33 grams | Protein: 13 grams | Sugar: 3 grams |

seed-crusted tuna
with sautéed greens

FOR 1 SERVING

Looking for a not-so-basic seafood dish? You've found it with this sesame-crusted tuna! The dressing for this dish uses tamari, a Japanese sauce made of fermented soybeans. It's thicker than soy sauce and has a more balanced, bold flavor. Tamari is often made without wheat, so it's a good gluten-free alternative. We also use tamari in our Teriyaki Edamame Turkey Meatballs (page 72).

DRESSING

1 tablespoon low-sodium tamari

1½ teaspoons toasted sesame oil

1½ teaspoons raw honey

1½ teaspoons rice vinegar

TUNA

2 tablespoons superfine almond flour

2 teaspoons black sesame seeds

2 teaspoons white sesame seeds

2 teaspoons hemp seeds

1 (6-ounce) pole-caught ahi tuna steak (about 1 inch thick)

1 teaspoon kosher salt

3 tablespoons avocado oil or cooking oil of choice

2 heads baby bok choy, halved through the root so they hold together

3 cups lightly packed Tuscan kale leaves, torn into bite-size pieces (about 8 leaves)

1 scallion, thinly sliced, for garnish

1. In a small bowl, whisk the dressing ingredients until the honey has dissolved. Set aside.

2. In a dish just larger than the tuna steak, combine the almond flour, sesame seeds, and hemp seeds.

3. Using a paper towel, pat the tuna steak dry on all sides. Season with salt on all sides. Lay the tuna steak in the dish with the seed mixture, pressing gently on all sides, including the edges to ensure it's evenly coated in a thick layer of seeds.

4. Heat a large cast-iron or stainless-steel skillet over medium-high. Add 2 tablespoons of the oil and swirl the pan. For rare to medium-rare tuna, add the steak to the pan when the oil is shimmering. Sear without touching for about 3 minutes. Flip and sear the other side until deep golden brown, 2 to 3 minutes more. Transfer to a plate and set aside to rest. If you like it more well-done, cook over medium heat for 1 to 2 minutes more per side. Carefully wipe out the pan.

5. Reduce the heat to medium. Add the remaining 1 tablespoon oil to the pan. Place the bok choy cut-side down in the pan and sprinkle the kale around and above them. Sear until the bok choy is deep golden brown and both vegetables start to soften, 2 to 3 minutes. Turn the bok choy over and stir the kale. Add half the dressing, about 1 tablespoon plus 1 teaspoon, to the pan and stir-fry the greens until tender-crisp, about 2 minutes.

6. Slice the tuna steak into strips and serve over the hot greens. Drizzle the tuna with the remaining dressing and top with the scallion.

NUTRITION, tuna, veggies, and 2 tablespoons dressing

| Calories: 809 | Carbs: 27 grams | Fiber: 9 grams |
| Fat: 52 grams | Protein: 64 grams | Sugar: 14 grams |

avocado-lime salmon

FOR 1 SERVING

Salmon is perfect for a quick solo meal. It cooks in under 20 minutes—and it's full of heart-healthy fats and omegas. Plus, cilantro is its perfect match—the vitamin K and calcium in cilantro help build strong bones and help to lower cholesterol and blood pressure. We know that cilantro can be a super divisive ingredient, so feel free to omit it if it's not your thing. Topped with our fresh avocado salsa, this dish is one you'll want time and again.

SALMON

6 ounces salmon, skin on or off

1 garlic clove, minced

1 teaspoon extra-virgin olive oil

Kosher salt and freshly ground black pepper

½ teaspoon paprika

AVOCADO SALSA

½ avocado, chopped (about ⅓ cup)

1 tablespoon finely chopped red onion

1½ teaspoons freshly chopped cilantro

1½ teaspoons extra-virgin olive oil

Kosher salt and freshly ground black pepper

Juice of ½ lime (about 1 tablespoon)

1. Preheat the oven to 400°F. Line a baking sheet with a reusable baking mat or parchment paper.

2. Place the salmon on the baking sheet skin-side down, if using skin-on. Season the salmon with the garlic, oil, salt, pepper, and paprika. Rub the fish on all sides to evenly distribute the seasonings.

3. Bake until soft and flaky, 8 to 12 minutes, or until cooked to your liking.

4. In a small bowl, mix together the avocado, red onion, cilantro, olive oil, salt, pepper, and lime juice. Don't overmix or you'll break down your avocado too much.

5. Let the salmon rest for 5 minutes before topping with the salsa and serving.

NUTRITION

| Calories: 763 | Carbs: 15 grams | Fiber: 8 grams |
| Fat: 61 grams | Protein: 40 grams | Sugar: 2 grams |

parchment-baked lemon and garlic chicken broccolini

FOR 1 SERVING

This entire meal cooks inside a parchment-paper pouch, meaning no pots and pans to clean up—a balanced meal without the fuss. Parchment paper is resistant to grease and moisture, which really makes the flavor of this chicken pop. The oh-so-trendy quinoa in this recipe is prepared and eaten like a grain, but it's actually a seed. It's gluten-free, high in protein, and loaded with fiber.

1 boneless skinless chicken breast, about 7 ounces

½ unwaxed lemon, thinly sliced into rounds (about ½ cup)

½ bunch of broccolini (4 or 5 stalks), dried ends trimmed

2 garlic cloves, smashed and peeled

½ medium shallot, thinly sliced into rounds (about ¼ cup)

2 sprigs thyme

2 teaspoons extra-virgin olive oil

2 tablespoons white wine or chicken stock

½ teaspoon kosher salt, plus more to taste

¼ teaspoon freshly ground black pepper, plus more to taste

½ cup cooked quinoa, about 3½ ounces

1. Preheat the oven to 375°F. Fold a 16 × 12-inch piece of parchment in half crosswise like a book, then open it again. Place the parchment on a baking sheet.

2. In a large bowl, combine the chicken, lemon slices, broccolini, garlic, shallots, thyme, olive oil, white wine, salt, and pepper. Toss to coat.

3. Spoon the quinoa in the middle of the parchment, just to the right of the fold, leaving a 2-inch border around the edges. Lay the seasoned vegetables and chicken on top of the quinoa and pour over any seasoning and juices in the bowl.

4. Fold the parchment in half over the chicken. Fold the bottom left corner (where the fold is) up about an inch, pressing along the fold to ensure it is tightly sealed. Move your hands slightly to the right and fold again. Keep moving along the edges to create a semicircle. On the last fold, tuck the last piece under the pouch to seal it.

5. Bake until the parchment parcel has puffed up and is turning golden brown, about 30 minutes. Let the pouch rest for 5 minutes before opening. Be careful when opening the pouch since there will still be a good amount of steam.

6. Season the chicken and vegetables with more salt and pepper and serve.

NUTRITION

| Calories: 625 | Carbs: 40 grams | Fiber: 9 grams |
| Fat: 19 grams | Protein: 69 grams | Sugar: 7 grams |

pumpkin and sage barley "risotto"

(V)

FOR 3 SERVINGS

This rustic risotto will leave you feeling warm and toasty inside. Canned pumpkin is available year-round, and this recipe uses the whole can of pumpkin—meaning no annoying half-can leftovers. Be sure to buy a can with a BPA-free lining. Pumpkin is high in vitamins A and C, which can strengthen your immune system. Leftovers make a great lunch later in the week. Enjoy!

1 tablespoon extra-virgin olive oil

1 small shallot, minced (about ½ cup)

1 garlic clove, minced

½ teaspoon kosher salt, plus more to taste

¼ teaspoon freshly ground black pepper, plus more to taste

4 cups low-sodium vegetable stock

1 cup pearled barley, about 6½ ounces

¼ cup dry white wine, such as Pinot Grigio or Sauvignon Blanc

1 (15-ounce) can pumpkin purée

6 small leaves fresh sage

½ cup frozen peas (optional)

1 to 2 tablespoons nutritional yeast or vegan Parmesan cheese (optional)

2 tablespoons pine nuts, toasted, for garnish

1. Heat a medium sauté pan with high sides or a Dutch oven over medium. Add the oil, shallot, garlic, salt, and pepper. Cook, stirring occasionally, until the shallot is soft and turning translucent, about 3 minutes.

2. Meanwhile, heat the vegetable stock in a small saucepan over medium. Keep the stock at a low simmer.

3. Add the barley to the pan with the shallot and garlic and stir. Toast, stirring frequently, until the barley is golden brown, 2 to 3 minutes. Pour in the white wine to deglaze the pan, scraping the pan to collect any bits into the sauce. Cook until the wine is almost evaporated, less than 1 minute.

4. Stir in the pumpkin purée and 3 whole sage leaves. Cook until the mixture is heated through and very thick, 1 to 2 minutes; there should be no excess liquid in the pan. If your brand of pumpkin purée has more liquid, you may need to cook the sauce down longer to make sure the sauce has the consistency of a thick paste before moving on.

5. While stirring, add 1 cup of the hot vegetable stock. Bring the mixture to a simmer and stir every few minutes until most of the liquid is absorbed, 7 to 8 minutes. You'll know it's time to add more liquid when there is a line left in the pan behind your spoon when you stir and the risotto bubbles look like lava. Repeat this process two more times, adding 1 cup of hot stock each time. When the risotto is thick again, add the remaining 1 cup hot stock and cook the liquid out, until the mixture is thick and the barley is tender. If the barley is not tender enough you can add 1 cup

RECIPE CONTINUES

hot water and simmer one more time until the liquid is reduced. Season with salt and pepper. Stir in the peas (if using) and heat through, 1 to 2 minutes.

6. Remove the pan from the heat and stir in the nutritional yeast (if using). Garnish with the remaining 3 sage leaves and the toasted pine nuts. Serve immediately. Reheat any leftovers on the stove by adding a splash of water (up to ¼ cup) and bringing it to a simmer, stirring until the liquid is reduced and the risotto is heated through.

NUTRITION

| Calories: 413 | Carbs: 59 grams | Fiber: 14 grams |
| Fat: 15 grams | Protein: 13 grams | Sugar: 14 grams |

one-pan roasted shrimp and zucchini "pappardelle"

FOR 1 SERVING

That's right—zoodles! This recipe replaces traditional pasta noodles with zucchini to keep the dish fresh and reduce the amount of carbs without sacrificing flavor. Zucchini is high in vitamin C, which builds collagen, helps iron absorption, and strengthens the immune system. This colorful dish looks as good as it tastes. We won't judge if you take a photo or two!

1 large zucchini

½ pound large shrimp, peeled, deveined, and tails removed (about 11 shrimp)

½ small yellow bell pepper, thinly sliced (about ¾ cup)

½ teaspoon kosher salt

¼ teaspoon freshly ground black pepper

¼ teaspoon garlic powder

1 tablespoon extra-virgin olive oil

Juice of ½ lemon (1½ tablespoons)

1. Preheat the oven to 400°F.

2. Using a vegetable peeler, peel long strips from the zucchini. Stop once you get to the seedy core, making about 1½ cups total. Compost or discard the core.

3. In a large bowl, mix the zucchini, shrimp, bell pepper, salt, black pepper, garlic powder, olive oil, and lemon juice until the shrimp and vegetables are evenly coated.

4. On a roasting pan, spread everything into one even layer and bake until the shrimp is pink and cooked through and the zucchini is slightly soft, 6 to 8 minutes.

5. Transfer to a serving bowl or plate and serve immediately.

NUTRITION

| Calories: 464 | Carbs: 20 grams | Fiber: 4 grams |
| Fat: 19 grams | Protein: 56 grams | Sugar: 8 grams |

halloumi and za'atar flatbread

FOR 1 SERVING

This thin and soft flatbread is just the right size for a meal for one. With a flavor similar to mozzarella, halloumi grilling cheese doesn't melt when heated, but instead attains a firm but silky smooth texture. When buying this cheese, compare sodium between brands and go for the lowest-sodium option. Za'atar is both an herb and a spice blend. The herb itself is hard to find, so this recipe will show you how to make your own Israeli-style spice blend at home.

ZA'ATAR SEASONING BLEND

1½ teaspoons toasted sesame seeds

1½ teaspoons ground sumac

1 teaspoon dried oregano

1 teaspoon dried thyme

1 teaspoon ground marjoram

1 teaspoon cumin

1½ teaspoons flaky sea salt

HALLOUMI AND FLATBREAD

2 tablespoons extra-virgin olive oil

1 piece store-bought whole-wheat naan or similar flatbread, about 9½ × 7 inches

3½ ounces halloumi cheese, torn into bite-size pieces (about ⅔ cup)

⅓ cup hummus, 3 ounces

½ English cucumber, sliced into rounds (heaping ¾ cup)

1 small heirloom or on-the-vine tomato, sliced into 5 or 6 slices

Kosher salt

1. Preheat the oven to 375°F. Line a baking sheet with a reusable baking mat or parchment paper.

2. In a small dish with a tight-fitting lid, combine the sesame seeds, sumac, oregano, thyme, marjoram, cumin, and salt.

3. Brush 1 tablespoon of the olive oil on both sides of the flatbread. Season one side with about 1 teaspoon of the za'atar. Place the oiled flatbread on the baking sheet seasoned-side up.

4. Bake the bread until lightly browned and aromatic, 5 to 7 minutes.

5. Heat a large cast-iron skillet over medium-high. Add the remaining 1 tablespoon oil to the pan and swirl to evenly distribute. Pat the halloumi pieces dry with a clean kitchen towel, then add to the hot pan and stir-fry until the halloumi is a crispy, deep golden brown on the outside, and soft on the inside, 1 to 2 minutes on each side. Return to the kitchen towel to cool slightly.

6. Remove the flatbread from the oven and allow to cool for 5 minutes.

7. Smear hummus over one side of the flatbread. Add the cucumber and tomato and season with salt. Top with the halloumi. Season with more za'atar. (Save the remaining za'atar in an airtight container for up to 6 months.) Cut the naan in half lengthwise and then in thirds crosswise so there are six pieces.

NUTRITION

Calories: 700	Carbs: 60 grams	Fiber: 9 grams
Fat: 42 grams	Protein: 35 grams	Sugar: 9 grams

braised mushrooms
with polenta

FOR 1 SERVING

Polenta, an Italian comfort food, is made from ground cornmeal and has the consistency of oatmeal or Cream of Wheat. It has a mild corn flavor but really takes on the flavors of whatever you cook it in. Our luscious mushroom gravy works with any type of mushroom you can find. Mushrooms are seasonal, so go to your local farmers' market and talk to the vendors—they are typically super knowledgeable and can point you to delicious, seasonal varieties. Or you can just choose your favorite—you'll never go wrong.

POLENTA

1⅓ cups water

¼ cup whole milk or milk of choice

1½ teaspoons kosher salt

¼ cup polenta or medium-grind yellow cornmeal

2 tablespoons unsalted grass-fed butter

2 tablespoons shredded Parmesan cheese

BRAISED MUSHROOMS

1 tablespoon avocado oil

12 ounces assorted mushrooms, such as oyster, cremini, and shiitake, cleaned and stemmed (about 3½ cups)

¾ teaspoon kosher salt, plus more to taste

2 tablespoons unsalted grass-fed butter

1 shallot, minced

1 garlic clove, minced

½ teaspoon freshly ground black pepper, plus more to taste

1 sprig thyme, or ½ teaspoon dried thyme, plus fresh thyme leaves for garnish

2 tablespoons Marsala wine

1 tablespoon whole-wheat all-purpose flour (use corn or rice flour for gluten-free)

¾ cup low-sodium vegetable or mushroom stock

1. Bring the water and milk to a boil in a medium saucepan. Once boiling, add the salt, stir with a whisk, and gradually pour in the polenta in a steady stream, stirring the entire time. Continue stirring until the polenta begins to thicken, about 2 minutes, then turn down the heat to low heat. Simmer gently until thick and tender, 35 to 40 minutes, stirring every 4 to 5 minutes to keep it from sticking. The mixture should be steaming and bubbling slightly the whole time.

2. While the polenta is cooking, make the mushrooms. Heat a large skillet over medium-high. Add the oil and swirl the pan to evenly distribute. When the oil is shimmering, add half the mushrooms to the skillet in an even layer and cook, undisturbed, until a crust forms on the bottom of the mushrooms, 2 to 3 minutes. Flip or stir the mushrooms, depending on your patience level. Season with ½ teaspoon of the salt and cook, undisturbed, for 2 to 3 minutes more. Remove the mushrooms from the pan and set aside on a plate to cool. Repeat the process with the remaining mushrooms.

3. Add the butter, shallot, garlic, remaining ¼ teaspoon salt, the pepper, and thyme to the empty skillet. Scrape up any mushroom bits from the bottom of the pan, stir, and cook until the shallot is soft and beginning to brown, 1 to 2 minutes.

4. Return the mushrooms to the pan and pour in the wine all at once. Bring the mixture to a boil, then stir and scrape up any bits from the skillet bottom. Continue to cook until almost all the wine has evaporated, 1 to 2 minutes.

5. Sprinkle the flour evenly over the vegetables and stir to coat until all the flour is absorbed. Toast the flour to cook out any raw flour taste, about 2 minutes.

6. Stirring constantly, gradually add the stock to the mushrooms. Bring to a boil and cook until the sauce is thick enough to coat the back of a spoon, 3 to 5 minutes. If overreduced, add more stock or water to loosen it to your preference. Taste and season with salt and pepper, if needed.

7. Once the polenta is tender, whisk in the butter and cheese. Taste and season with salt and pepper if needed.

8. Serve the braised mushrooms over the polenta and garnish with thyme leaves. Serve immediately. If you have any leftovers, store them in an airtight container in the refrigerator for up to 5 days. When reheating, add a splash of water to the polenta to loosen it up.

NUTRITION

| Calories: 788 | Carbs: 35 grams | Fiber: 9 grams |
| Fat: 69 grams | Protein: 15 grams | Sugar: 14 grams |

fig and cannellini salad
with honeyed walnuts

FOR 2 SERVINGS

The blend of figs, lettuce, beans, and nuts makes for a colorful and impressive salad. The beans and walnuts add fiber and protein to this elegant salad. Endive is slightly bitter but crisp and refreshing, and any harshness is offset by the sweet honey in the dressing. Figs are in season during the summer, so in the fall, try this salad with persimmons, grapes, or apples. In the winter, try a D'Anjou pear, and in the spring, sprinkle with apricots and berries.

VINAIGRETTE

1 tablespoon raw honey

2 teaspoons white wine vinegar

1½ teaspoons Dijon mustard

2 tablespoons extra-virgin olive oil

Kosher salt and freshly ground black pepper

HONEYED WALNUTS

½ tablespoon unsalted grass-fed butter

1 tablespoon raw honey

⅓ cup roughly chopped walnut halves, about 1½ ounces

SALAD

1 (15-ounce) can no-salt-added cannellini beans, drained and rinsed

1 head endive

4 leaves butter lettuce, torn into bite-size pieces (about 2 cups)

3 figs, quartered

Kosher salt and freshly ground black pepper

¼ cup shaved Parmesan cheese

1. In a medium bowl, whisk together the honey, vinegar, and mustard. While whisking, add the oil in a steady stream and continue to whisk until the dressing is emulsified. Season with salt and pepper. Set aside.

2. Heat a small frying pan over medium. Melt the butter and honey, mixing until evenly combined. When the mixture just starts to bubble, stir in the walnuts. Cook until the walnuts are toasted and the sauce reduces to coat the walnuts, 2 to 3 minutes. Remove from the pan.

3. Without wiping out the pan, turn the heat to low. Add the cannellini beans and about half the vinaigrette, then turn the heat to medium-low. Stir occasionally until just heated through and the sauce thickens slightly, 2 to 3 minutes. Season with salt and pepper. Set aside.

4. Peel off any endive leaves that are brown or wilted. Cut the endive in half and remove the core. Add the endive leaves to the bowl with the remaining vinaigrette.

5. Add the lettuce, honeyed walnuts, cannellini beans, and figs. Season with salt and pepper. Serve topped with the shaved Parmesan.

NUTRITION, per serving (salad only)

| Calories: 625 | Carbs: 81 grams | Fiber: 16 grams |
| Fat: 30 grams | Protein: 20 grams | Sugar: 44 grams |

NUTRITION, per 2 tablespoons dressing

| Calories: 315 | Carbs: 19 grams | Fiber: 1 gram |
| Fat: 27 grams | Protein: 1 gram | Sugar: 17 grams |

soy and sesame crispy eggplant

FOR 1 SERVING

This purple veggie is a powerhouse: It contains nasunin, an antioxidant that improves blood flow to the brain, as well as fiber, potassium, vitamin C, and vitamin B_6, which supports heart health. Our sweet-and-salty marinade pairs with eggplant perfectly and can also be used on any of your other favorite veggies. You can add these to the baking sheet, topped with the marinade, when broiling. Eat this dish with brown rice on the side, and voilà, you've got an amazing meal.

1 medium Italian eggplant, about 1 pound

½ teaspoon kosher salt

2 tablespoons avocado oil

½ inch fresh ginger, grated

1 garlic clove, grated

1 tablespoon low-sodium soy sauce

1 teaspoon dark sesame seed oil (the darker the color, the stronger the flavor)

1 tablespoon raw honey

1 teaspoon unseasoned rice vinegar

Toasted sesame seeds, for garnish

Fresh cilantro, for garnish

1 cup steamed brown rice, for serving

1. Remove the top of the eggplant and slice in half lengthwise. Using a sharp paring knife, cut diagonal lines into the flesh every ½ inch or so, going about ½ inch deep. Repeat the lines in the opposite direction, creating a crosshatch pattern. Repeat with the remaining eggplant half.

2. Season the eggplant with the salt and let sit for about 10 minutes.

3. Meanwhile, in a shallow 9 × 9-inch baking dish (it should be slightly bigger than the eggplant), whisk together the avocado oil, ginger, garlic, soy sauce, sesame oil, honey, and rice vinegar.

4. Adjust the oven rack about 8 inches from the broiler source, then preheat the broiler to high. Line a baking sheet with a reusable baking mat or parchment paper.

5. Using a clean kitchen towel or a paper towel, firmly press on the cut sides of the eggplant to remove as much excess moisture as possible. Lay the eggplant flesh-side down in the marinade and let sit for 10 minutes.

6. Place the eggplant flesh-side up on the baking sheet and pour half the marinade over the top. Gently pull on the sides of the eggplant to open the crosshatch marks so the marinade goes deep into the eggplant. Broil for 4 to 5 minutes, then rotate the pan and spoon the remaining marinade on the eggplant. Broil until the eggplant flesh is fork-tender and the sauce is caramelized over the top, making it a deep golden brown, 4 to 5 minutes more.

7. Garnish with sesame seeds and cilantro. Serve immediately over the steamed brown rice.

NUTRITION

Calories: 591	Carbs: 105 grams	Fiber: 16 grams
Fat: 18 grams	Protein: 10 grams	Sugar: 32 grams

one-pan pancetta and basil–wrapped chicken breast

with roasted sweet potatoes

FOR 1 SERVING

This recipe takes chicken to new heights with crispy, salty pancetta, unsmoked Italian bacon. Even better, the sweet potato is baked until it's crunchy on the outside and soft and sweet on the inside. This savory dish is loaded with protein, fiber, potassium, and complex carbs, making it nourishing and tasty all at the same time. We use parchment paper here for hassle-free cleanup.

1 sweet potato, scrubbed and cut into ½-inch pieces (about 2 heaping cups)

2 tablespoons avocado oil

1 sprig fresh thyme, or ½ teaspoon dried thyme

2 garlic cloves, skin-on, slightly smashed

1 teaspoon kosher salt

½ teaspoon freshly ground black pepper

1 boneless, skinless chicken breast, about 7 ounces

2 basil leaves, plus more for garnish

1 thin slice pancetta, about 1 ounce

1. Preheat the oven to 375°F. Line a baking sheet with a reusable baking mat or parchment paper.

2. Add the sweet potato to the baking sheet and toss with the avocado oil, thyme, garlic, ½ teaspoon of the salt, and ¼ teaspoon of the pepper. Spread the potato pieces out in an even layer, leaving a space in the middle for the chicken.

3. Season the chicken on both sides with the remaining salt and pepper and place on the baking sheet. Lay the basil leaves on the chicken, then top with the pancetta, tucking the edges underneath the chicken breast.

4. Bake until the potato is tender, the chicken is cooked through, and the pancetta is crispy, 30 to 35 minutes. If the pancetta isn't crispy when the potato is done, remove the potato to a plate and preheat your broiler to high. Crisp the pancetta under the broiler until the fat is rendered and the pancetta is golden brown, 1 to 2 minutes.

5. Peel the garlic and smash the flesh into a paste. Toss the potato with the garlic paste and plate the potato pieces alongside the chicken. Garnish with the crispy thyme leaves and fresh basil. Serve immediately.

NUTRITION

| Calories: 858 | Carbs: 33 grams | Fiber: 5 grams |
| Fat: 50 grams | Protein: 67 grams | Sugar: 10 grams |

bad-day carbonara

FOR 1 SERVING

Sometimes it's just one of those days when you want to make yourself a warm bowl of carbonara and sit on the couch. No judgments here, we've got you! The good thing about carbonara is that you might already have the ingredients in your fridge, since they're all pretty long-lasting essentials. The pasta and the sauce both cook in around the same amount of time so you won't have to wait. Relax, you've got this!

2 tablespoons kosher salt, plus more to season cooking water

4 ounces uncooked chickpea spaghetti

1 teaspoon extra-virgin olive oil

2 thin slices pancetta, about 1½ ounces, or 1 slice uncured bacon, cut into ¼-inch cubes

1 free-range large egg, room temperature

1 free-range egg yolk, room temperature

1 teaspoon freshly ground black pepper

¼ cup freshly grated Parmigiano-Reggiano cheese, about 1 ounce, plus more for serving

2 tablespoons roughly chopped flat-leaf parsley, for garnish

1. Bring a large pot of water to a boil over high heat. Season the water generously with salt when it begins to simmer so the salt dissolves.

2. Add the pasta to the boiling water and stir to avoid sticking. Cook for 2 minutes less than the time indicated on the package. The pasta should be tender enough that it bends but still have a strong al dente bite to it. The pasta will finish cooking in the sauce at the end.

3. Place a large, tall frying pan over medium heat. Add the oil and heat for about 1 minute. Add the pancetta and sauté until golden brown and just turning crispy, stirring frequently, about 3 minutes. Remove the pan from the heat and set aside; the pancetta will continue to crisp as it cools.

4. In a small bowl or 1-cup liquid measuring cup, whisk the egg with the egg yolk. Add the pepper and half the cheese. Stir to combine.

5. Check the pasta for doneness. Reserve 1 cup of the pasta cooking liquid, then drain the pasta.

6. Add the pasta and ½ cup of the reserved pasta water to the pan with the pancetta.

7. Add the egg mixture to the pan and quickly begin stirring and shaking the pan to avoid scrambling the eggs. Make sure the egg mixture and the hot pasta water are evenly combined; this will temper the eggs. Place the pot back over medium-low heat and cook, stirring constantly, until the sauce thickens and coats the pasta, about 3 minutes. The sauce should be rich and silky. Remove from the heat.

8. Sprinkle with the remaining cheese and stir until the cheese is melted. Garnish with the parsley and serve immediately.

NUTRITION

| Calories: 920 | Carbs: 91 grams | Fiber: 4 grams |
| Fat: 45 grams | Protein: 35 grams | Sugar: 3 grams |

summer tomato pasta

FOR 1 SERVING

This is one of those cases where simplicity really is key. With just a few fresh ingredients, this luscious pasta is vibrant and light. The dish shines when you use truly ripe summer tomatoes (a bargain at the market in July and August).

Kosher salt

3 or 4 vine-ripened tomatoes, about 1 pound

2 tablespoons good-quality extra-virgin olive oil

2 garlic cloves, minced

¼ cup packed torn basil, about 6 leaves, plus more for garnish

½ teaspoon crushed red pepper flakes

¼ teaspoon freshly ground black pepper, plus more to taste

4 ounces uncooked chickpea spaghetti

¼ cup freshly grated Parmesan cheese (optional)

1. Bring a large pot of water to a boil. When the water is simmering, add a generous amount of salt, enough so that the water tastes like the ocean. Have a medium bowl filled with ice water nearby.

2. Cut a small "X" in the bottom of the tomatoes. Once the water is boiling, add the tomatoes and blanch until you see the skin peeling away from the flesh, 40 to 60 seconds.

3. Remove the tomatoes from the hot water using a slotted spoon and immediately plunge them into the ice water.

4. Remove the tomatoes from the ice water. When cool enough to handle, peel off the skins and compost or discard.

5. Cut the tomatoes into quarters and remove the core and most of the seeds. Roughly dice the tomatoes into ¼-inch dice, about 2 cups. Place in a large bowl with the oil, garlic, basil, red pepper flakes, 1 teaspoon salt, and the black pepper. Stir to coat. Marinate for 30 minutes, stirring halfway through.

6. Add more water to the water you used to blanch the tomatoes, if needed, and bring back to a boil. Cook the spaghetti according to the package directions, then drain the pasta.

7. Add the spaghetti to the tomatoes and stir to coat the pasta in the sauce. Add the Parmesan (if using). Let sit and soak up the liquid released from the tomatoes for 1 to 2 minutes. Stir once more, top with extra basil, and serve.

NUTRITION

| Calories: 773 | Carbs: 106 grams | Fiber: 9 grams |
| Fat: 31 grams | Protein: 21 grams | Sugar: 15 grams |

sips

"

Listen to yourself.
What is it that you need?
Do you need to slow
down? Are you yearning
for motivation to keep
up your momentum?

"

drink up

This chapter is a fun mix of beverage recipes to keep you hydrated and your palate whet: teas to help when you're feeling under the weather, cocktails to be enjoyed with or without alcohol, and some of our favorite nutrient-packed smoothies.

veggie-packed smoothies

FOR 2 SERVINGS EACH

steps for veggie-packed smoothies

1. Place all the ingredients except the ice and honey (if using) in a blender or food processor and blend until just combined.

2. Add the ice and blend until smooth. Blend in honey (if using).

strawberry ginger beet

This vibrant red blend of strawberries, ginger, and beets is full of amazing vitamins that will make you feel refreshed and revived.

1 cup sliced strawberries

1½ cups lightly packed sliced romaine lettuce

½ red beet, peeled and diced

1 inch fresh ginger, peeled

1½ cups ice

Raw honey (optional)

NUTRITION, per serving

| Calories: 117 | Carbs: 27 grams | Fiber: 6 grams |
| Fat: 1 gram | Protein: 3 grams | Sugar: 18 grams |

blueberry banana spinach

This smoothie is an easy way to get your daily serving of greens. The blueberries and banana make it sweet.

1 cup blueberries,

1 cup lightly packed baby spinach

1 banana, chopped

1½ cups ice

NUTRITION, per serving

| Calories: 102 | Carbs: 26 grams | Fiber: 4 grams |
| Fat: 1 gram | Protein: 2 grams | Sugar: 15 grams |

cucumber apple mint

The secret ingredient, avocado, gives it a smooth, milkshake-like creaminess.

½ large cucumber, peeled and sliced

¼ cup lightly packed mint leaves

1 green apple, such as Granny Smith, cored and diced

1 tablespoon raw honey, plus more to taste

½ avocado, diced

1½ cups ice

NUTRITION, per serving

| Calories: 148 | Carbs: 27 grams | Fiber: 5 grams |
| Fat: 5 grams | Protein: 1 gram | Sugar: 19 grams |

anti-inflammatory golden turmeric milk

FOR 2 SERVINGS; MAKES 2 CUPS

This comforting golden milk gets its signature color from turmeric. Turmeric is a spice that contains curcumin, which reduces inflammation. Eastern medicinal practices have been recommending golden turmeric milk for centuries! In recent years, we've been able to scientifically connect turmeric with all sorts of health benefits. Plus, golden milk is calming before bed. Drink this and you're pretty much guaranteed a night of sweet dreams.

2 cups unsweetened almond milk or milk of choice

1 tablespoon ground turmeric

¼ teaspoon ground ginger

4 black peppercorns

1 cinnamon stick

1 star anise

Pinch of whole cloves (about 4)

Raw honey or sweetener of choice (optional)

1. Pour the almond milk into a small pot over medium heat. Add the turmeric, ginger, peppercorns, cinnamon, star anise, and cloves. Whisk to combine.

2. Heat the milk until steaming, but do not let it come to a boil, 4 to 6 minutes.

3. Strain and serve warm or over ice. Sweeten as desired.

NUTRITION, per serving

| Calories: 91 | Carbs: 17 grams | Fiber: 3 grams |
| Fat: 3 grams | Protein: 2 grams | Sugar: 9 grams |

sparkling tonics

Each of these bubbly tonics is great with a refreshing seltzer or a sparkling wine of your choice. These tonics are crowd-pleasers either way. Make these the next time you're hosting and we're sure everyone will be impressed. Note that some wines are not vegan because they contain casein, a dairy protein.

mint and celery tonic

FOR 3 SERVINGS

Mint is a soothing herb that calms an upset stomach and is good for digestion. Coconut sugar is less processed than granulated sugar and balances the sour taste of the lemon juice. Combine these simple ingredients with celery juice and you have a refreshing, mild, low-sugar drink.

1 bunch organic celery, root end removed

3 sprigs fresh mint, plus more for garnish

1½ teaspoons coconut sugar

3 teaspoons freshly squeezed lemon juice

24 ounces sparkling water or wine

1. Thoroughly clean the celery. Roughly chop about 4½ cups, leaving a handful of the top leaves as garnish for later. Add the celery to a blender and blend on high until completely smooth, about 90 seconds.

2. Strain the celery through cheesecloth or a fine-mesh strainer over a large liquid measuring cup. Press the fibrous material into the strainer to get all the liquid out of it. (This makes about 1½ cups.)

3. To serve, add the leaves of 1 sprig of mint to a glass with ½ teaspoon of the sugar and 1 teaspoon of the lemon juice. Muddle with the handle of a wooden spoon and pour in ½ cup of the celery juice along with 6 to 8 ounces of the sparkling beverage of your choice. Repeat with the remaining two glasses. Garnish with the celery leaves and mint sprigs.

NUTRITION, per serving (with seltzer)

| Calories: 35 | Carbs: 8 grams | Fiber: 3 grams |
| Fat: 0 grams | Protein: 0 grams | Sugar: 5 grams |

NUTRITION, per serving (with wine)

| Calories: 179 | Carbs: 12 grams | Fiber: 3 grams |
| Fat: 0 grams | Protein: 2 grams | Sugar: 6 grams |

fizzy rosemary and honeyed lemonade

FOR 8 SERVINGS

When life hands you lemons, make the best lemonade you've ever tasted. This is a modern twist on the classic refreshment. Rosemary adds a surprising flavor to lemonade with its sage-like, peppery, woody taste.

2½ cups water

½ cup raw honey

11 sprigs rosemary

1 cup freshly squeezed lemon juice
(from about 4 large unwaxed lemons)

48 ounces sparkling water or wine,
about 1½ liters

1 unwaxed lemon, sliced into 8 rounds,
for garnish

1. Heat a small saucepan over medium. Add
½ cup of the water and the honey, and stir until
the honey is dissolved, about 3 minutes. Add
3 rosemary sprigs. Turn off the heat and steep for
15 minutes.

2. Strain the rosemary-honey syrup into a pitcher
and add the lemon juice and remaining 2 cups
water.

3. Pour ½ cup of the rosemary-honey lemonade
and 6 to 8 ounces of the sparkling beverage of
your choice into each glass and adorn with a
lemon round and a sprig of rosemary.

NUTRITION, per serving (with seltzer)

| Calories: 77 | Carbs: 21 grams | Fiber: 1 gram |
| Fat: 0 grams | Protein: 0 grams | Sugar: 18 grams |

NUTRITION, per serving (with wine)

| Calories: 221 | Carbs: 25 grams | Fiber: 1 gram |
| Fat: 0 grams | Protein: 0 grams | Sugar: 20 grams |

hibiscus coconut fizz

FOR 8 SERVINGS

This fruity drink is tart yet fragrant and
sweet, smooth yet bubbly.

1 cup water

⅓ cup agave nectar

6 bags hibiscus tea

1 cup blueberries

1½ cups full-fat unsweetened coconut milk,
well mixed before measuring

48 ounces sparkling water or wine, about
1½ liters

1. In a small saucepan, bring the water to a boil.
Turn off the heat, stir in the agave, add the tea bags,
and steep for 8 minutes. Remove the tea bags.

2. Place the sweetened tea and blueberries in a
blender and mix on high until very smooth, 3 to
4 minutes. (This makes about 1¾ cups.)

3. To serve, add ¼ cup of the blueberry purée and
¼ cup of the coconut milk to a glass. Add 6 to
8 ounces of the sparkling beverage and gently stir.

NUTRITION, per serving (with seltzer)

| Calories: 49 | Carbs: 10 grams | Fiber: 0 grams |
| Fat: 9 grams | Protein: 0 grams | Sugar: 8 grams |

NUTRITION, per serving (with sparkling wine)

| Calories: 193 | Carbs: 15 grams | Fiber: 0 grams |
| Fat: 9 grams | Protein: 0 grams | Sugar: 10 grams |

4 immunity-boosting drinks

green vitamin juice

The spinach and kale in this juice are nutritional powerhouses. They're rich in vitamin C, one of the top immunity boosters. This green juice will help keep your immune system strong all year long.

1½ cups freshly squeezed orange juice

1 cup lightly packed baby spinach

1 cup stemmed kale leaves

½ cucumber, sliced

1 small apple, cored and diced

Orange slices, for garnish (optional)

1. Combine the orange juice, spinach, and kale in a blender and blend until smooth.

2. Add the cucumber and apple. Blend until smooth.

3. Pour into a glass and serve right away, or chill in the refrigerator. Garnish with an orange slice, if desired.

NUTRITION, per serving

| Calories: 154 | Carbs: 38 grams | Fiber: 4 grams |
| Fat: 0 grams | Protein: 4 grams | Sugar: 27 grams |

probiotic berry smoothie

Made with kefir, this smoothie is packed with probiotics to help with digestion. Kefir is a fermented milk drink, cultured from kefir grains, that tastes like plain tart yogurt.

1½ cups milk of choice

1 cup whole-milk kefir

1½ cups frozen strawberries

1½ cups frozen blueberries

Combine the milk, kefir, strawberries, and blueberries in a blender and blend until smooth.

NUTRITION, per serving

| Calories: 276 | Carbs: 42 grams | Fiber: 6 grams |
| Fat: 8 grams | Protein: 11 grams | Sugar: 22 grams |

veggie tomato juice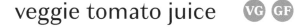

This is a great substitute for canned or bottled tomato juice, which can be high in sodium. Red bell peppers and tomatoes are excellent sources of vitamin C. Add a couple dashes of hot sauce to make it a Bloody Mary mix.

4 tomatoes, diced

1 large carrot, sliced

1 large celery stalk, sliced, plus more for optional garnish

1 medium red bell pepper, diced

Kosher salt and freshly ground black pepper

1 tablespoon minced garlic

½ cup water

2 tablespoons freshly chopped flat-leaf parsley

1. Place the tomatoes, carrot, celery, bell pepper, garlic, salt, water, and black pepper in a large pot and bring to a boil.

2. Reduce the heat, cover, and simmer until the vegetables are tender, about 20 minutes.

3. Remove from the heat and let cool for about 10 minutes.

4. Transfer the mixture to a blender and add the parsley. Remove the small cap from the lid of the blender and then cover the opening with a kitchen towel. This will help to release excess steam while blending. Blend on high speed until smooth. Alternatively, use an immersion blender and purée the vegetable mixture directly in the pot after cooling. Thin with cold water if the juice is too thick. Serve chilled. Garnish with a celery stalk, if desired.

NUTRITION, per serving

| Calories: 91 | Carbs: 15 grams | Fiber: 4 grams |
| Fat: 0 grams | Protein: 2 grams | Sugar: 7 grams |

soothing lemon ginger tea

Make a cup of this tea in the morning to start your day or at night to wind down. Lemon and ginger both help to fight infections and can shorten the length of colds and flus. This is the right choice if you've been feeling under the weather. Get well soon!

4 cups water

1 large unwaxed lemon, plus lemon slices for optional garnish

2 to 3 inches fresh ginger

2 teaspoons raw honey or sweetener of choice

1. Bring the water to a boil in a medium saucepan and remove from the heat.

2. Cut the lemon and ginger into thin slices. Add to the hot water and steep for 5 minutes.

3. Strain the tea into a mug. Add the honey, stir, and serve. Garnish with a lemon slice, if desired.

NUTRITION, per serving

| Calories: 76 | Carbs: 21 grams | Fiber: 2 grams |
| Fat: 1 gram | Protein: 2 grams | Sugar: 9 grams |

energy smoothies

avocado cold brew

FOR 4 SERVINGS

We're combining two beloved ingredients in this tantalizing beverage: avocado and coffee. The vanilla yogurt and avocado make this blended beverage super creamy and dreamy. The coconut milk has no cholesterol and adds a subtle coconut flavor that is divine. Sprinkle coconut flakes on top to finish!

½ cup cold-brew coffee

½ avocado, chopped

1 tablespoon pure vanilla extract

1 cup full-fat unsweetened coconut milk, mixed well before measuring

½ cup unsweetened vanilla yogurt, about 5 ounces

2 cups ice

Raw honey (optional)

Coconut flakes, for garnish

Place the coffee, avocado, vanilla, coconut milk, yogurt, and ice in a blender. Blend until smooth. Blend in honey to sweeten, if desired. Serve in a glass, topped with coconut flakes.

NUTRITION, per 1-cup serving

Calories: 248	Carbs: 28 grams	Fiber: 4 grams
Fat: 14 grams	Protein: 3 grams	Sugar: 22 grams

cinnamon oatmeal smoothie

FOR 4 SERVINGS

This filling, cinnamon-flavored smoothie is a meal in a glass, and has all the ingredients of a balanced breakfast: oats, yogurt, banana, and coffee. Not all oats are gluten-free. Be sure to read the package.

1 banana, sliced

½ cup rolled oats

½ cup unsweetened vanilla yogurt

1 teaspoon cinnamon, plus more for serving

1 tablespoon raw honey

1 cup brewed coffee, cooled

1 cup unsweetened cashew milk

2 cups ice

Combine all the ingredients in a blender. Blend on high speed until smooth. Divide among four glasses and top with a sprinkle of cinnamon.

NUTRITION, per 1-cup serving

Calories: 162	Carbs: 33 grams	Fiber: 3 grams
Fat: 2 grams	Protein: 5 grams	Sugar: 18 grams

banana matcha

FOR 2 SERVINGS

Banana and almond milk are the perfect matcha! A green tea that gives you three times the caffeine of a cup of steeped tea, matcha will still make you feel calm. The spinach adds iron and other nutrients that will keep you moving all day long.

1 banana, sliced

1 tablespoon matcha powder, plus more for serving

1 cup unsweetened almond milk

1 cup lightly packed baby spinach

2 cups ice

Raw honey or agave nectar (optional)

Combine the banana, matcha, almond milk, spinach, and ice in a blender. Blend until smooth. Blend in honey to sweeten, if desired. Divide between two glasses and top with a sprinkle of matcha powder.

NUTRITION, per 1½-cup serving

| Calories: 126 | Carbs: 29 grams | Fiber: 3 grams |
| Fat: 2 grams | Protein: 2 grams | Sugar: 19 grams |

anti-inflammatory cantaloupe and mint juice

FOR 4 SERVINGS; MAKES ABOUT 5½ CUPS

Try having a spa day at home in the near future with this lovely beverage. With a 90 percent water content, cantaloupe is a super hydrator and has the added benefits of beta-carotene, vitamin A, vitamin C, and potassium. Mint has anti-inflammatory compounds—and the combination just tastes heavenly.

1 ripe cantaloupe melon, about 3½ pounds

Leaves from 3 sprigs mint (about ¼ cup)

1 cup cold water

1. Wash the melon. Cut off the top and bottom and lay one of the flat sides down on a cutting board. Cut off the rind in strips from top to bottom, rotating the melon until all the rind is removed. Slice the melon in half and use a spoon to remove the seeds and inner membrane.

2. Cut the melon into chunks (you'll have about 6 cups) and place in a blender. Add the mint and water to the blender.

3. Blend on high until smooth, about 30 seconds. Serve chilled or over ice.

NUTRITION, per serving

| Calories: 141 | Carbs: 34 grams | Fiber: 4 grams |
| Fat: 1 gram | Protein: 3 grams | Sugar: 32 grams |

spicy avocado mezcal margarita

FOR 2 SERVINGS

So it's happy hour, is it? Great! This sweet-and-sour drink will take you to the sandy beaches of Cancún—whether or not you use the tequila. The avocado gives it a nice creamy thickness (plus some heart-healthy fats), and the jalapeño adds just the right amount of heat. Cheers!

1 avocado, pitted and peeled

1 small jalapeño, seeded and roughly chopped (about 2 tablespoons) plus 4 jalapeño slices, for garnish

⅓ cup freshly squeezed lime juice (from about 3 large limes)

¼ cup freshly squeezed orange juice (from about ½ large navel orange)

¼ cup agave nectar

½ cup ice

⅓ cup mezcal, tequila blanco, or water

2 lime wedges, for garnish

Combine the avocado, jalapeño, lime juice, orange juice, agave, ice, and mezcal in a blender. Blend on high until smooth, about 30 seconds. Serve immediately, garnished with jalapeño slices and lime wedges.

NUTRITION, per serving (with alcohol)

| Calories: 345 | Carbs: 37 grams | Fiber: 7 grams |
| Fat: 16 grams | Protein: 2 grams | Sugar: 23 grams |

NUTRITION, per serving (without alcohol)

| Calories: 279 | Carbs: 37 grams | Fiber: 7 grams |
| Fat: 16 grams | Protein: 2 grams | Sugar: 23 grams |

frozen bloody mary

FOR 16 SERVINGS

This veggie-packed Bloody Mary is a nutritious way to enjoy a cocktail. Tomato juice is rich in vitamins and antioxidants, and the horseradish can boost the immune system, aid digestion, fight bacteria, and relieve respiratory conditions. Make a batch of this a day ahead to ease party-hosting anxiety.

4 cups low-sodium tomato juice

3 tablespoons packed freshly grated peeled horseradish, or prepared horseradish to taste

Juice of 1 lemon (about ¼ cup)

2 tablespoons Worcestershire sauce (vegan options available)

¼ cup olive brine or pickle juice

1 to 2 tablespoons hot sauce

1½ teaspoons freshly ground black pepper

1½ teaspoons celery salt

1½ teaspoons celery seed

2 English cucumbers, sliced (4½ cups)

1 pound vine-ripened tomatoes, about 4 medium, roughly chopped (3 cups)

32 ounces vodka (optional)

1 unwaxed lemon, cut into wedges, for garnish

1. The night before serving, in a large pitcher, place the tomato juice, horseradish, lemon juice, Worcestershire, olive brine, hot sauce, pepper, celery salt, and celery seed. Stir to combine, and refrigerate.

2. Place the cucumbers and tomatoes on a small baking sheet and freeze overnight. Once the cucumbers and tomatoes are frozen, you can store them in a reusable plastic bag in the freezer to have on hand for future Bloody Marys (or to use in gazpacho or smoothies).

3. To serve, in a blender, combine 1 cup of the frozen cucumbers and 1 cup of the frozen tomatoes with 2 cups of the Bloody Mary mix. Add ½ cup of vodka (if using). Blend until smooth. Pour into four glasses and repeat. Serve each drink with a lemon wedge. Garnish with anything you have in the fridge: pickles, olives, celery stalks, cucumber rounds. Have fun with it!

NUTRITION, per serving (with alcohol)

| Calories: 152 | Carbs: 5 grams | Fiber: 1 gram |
| Fat: 1 gram | Protein: 1 gram | Sugar: 3 grams |

NUTRITION, per serving (without alcohol)

| Calories: 23 | Carbs: 5 grams | Fiber: 1 gram |
| Fat: 1 gram | Protein: 1 gram | Sugar: 3 grams |

hot toddy

FOR 1 SERVING

A warm hot toddy is always there for whatever ails you. Liquor is traditionally used in a hot toddy, but it's totally optional. This perfect combination of herbal tea, honey, lemon, and steam will help to clear your sinuses and put your mind at ease.

1½ cups just-boiled water

1 bag herbal tea, such as chamomile, ginger root, rose hip, tulsi (holy basil), echinacea, orange peel, lemon peel, spearmint, or lemongrass

1 cinnamon stick

1 star anise

2 teaspoons raw honey

2 tablespoons freshly squeezed lemon juice

1½ ounces brown liquor, such as brandy, whiskey, or dark rum (3 tablespoons; optional)

1. Pour the hot water into a mug and add the tea bag, cinnamon, and star anise. Steep for 2 to 3 minutes, or according to the package directions. Remove and discard the tea bag.

2. Stir in the honey until it dissolves. Add the lemon juice and the liquor (if using).

3. Turn off any screens that omit a blue light (these can inhibit good sleep patterns), snuggle under a blanket, and get some rest.

NUTRITION, per serving (with whiskey)

Calories: 149	Carbs: 14 grams	Fiber: 0 grams
Fat: 0 grams	Protein: 0 grams	Sugar: 12 grams

classic matcha latte

FOR 1 SERVING

Learning how to make your favorite drinks at home is fun, rewarding, and practical. You can treat yourself more regularly and keep your monthly budget in check. Soon enough, you'll be making matcha lattes at home! Matcha boosts metabolism, detoxifies, and can enhance your mood. You'll want to make one for you and one for your bestie too.

¾ cup grass-fed whole milk or milk of choice (dairy milk froths better)

¾ teaspoon matcha powder

½ teaspoon cold water

1. Boil a fresh pot of water. Measure out ¾ cup into a jug and set aside to cool for 2 minutes—if the water is too hot, it will scorch the matcha, leaving an unpleasant bitter taste.

2. Pour the milk into a mason jar and tightly close the lid. Shake until almost doubled in volume, about 1 minute. Remove the lid and microwave for 30 seconds.

3. In your latte mug, dissolve the matcha in the cold water to form a paste. Add the hot water to the matcha paste and vigorously whisk from side to side, rotating the mug to evenly aerate the tea and ensure the matcha paste is dissolved in the water.

4. Using a spoon to hold back the milk froth, pour the warm milk into the mug. Top the latte with the frothed milk. Perfect matcha latte.

NUTRITION

| Calories: 112 | Carbs: 9 grams | Fiber: 0 grams |
| Fat: 6 grams | Protein: 6 grams | Sugar: 9 grams |

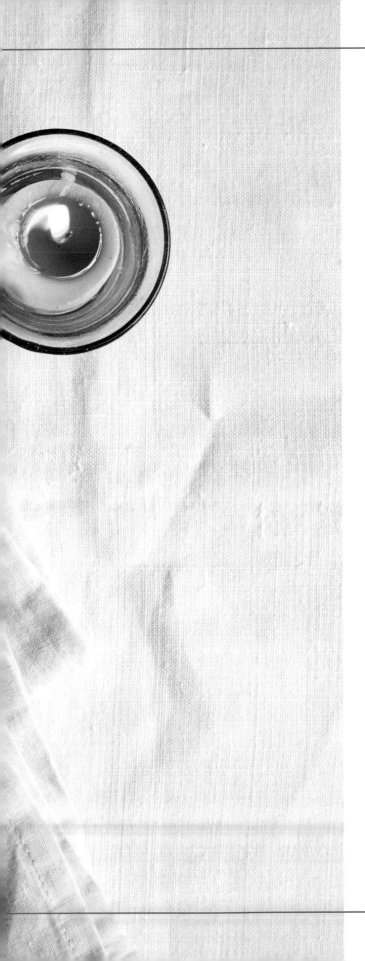

evenings

"

It's incredibly soothing
and rewarding to watch
ingredients become
something delicious
that nourishes you.

"

good evening!

Dinnertime shouldn't have to be synonymous with stress. This chapter includes easy, scrumptious meals that won't wear you out after a long, busy day. These recipes are also great for sharing. No matter which dish you choose to make, we hope it's a gratifying way to wrap up your day.

stuffed poblano peppers

FOR 6 SERVINGS

This meatless meal brings the heat. The health benefits of poblano chilies come from an active ingredient called capsaicin. This makes the peppers hot, but it also lowers cholesterol and blood pressure. Poblanos bring more of a kick than bell peppers, but bell work just as well.

6 large poblano chilies

1 tablespoon extra-virgin olive oil or cooking oil of choice

½ red onion, finely diced

Kosher salt

3 garlic cloves, minced

2 teaspoons cumin

1 teaspoon ground coriander

⅛ teaspoon cayenne pepper

2 cups cooked quinoa

1 (14.5-ounce) can no-salt-added black beans, drained and rinsed

5 ounces canned tomato sauce (about ⅔ cup)

Juice of ½ lime (about 1 tablespoon), plus lime wedges for serving

¼ cup roughly chopped fresh cilantro, plus more for serving

¾ cup shredded Monterey Jack cheese

Avocado slices, for serving

1. Preheat the oven to 425°F. Line a baking sheet.

2. Roast the whole poblanos on the baking sheet until the skin begins to brown and pull away from the flesh of the pepper, about 20 minutes.

3. Meanwhile, in a large sauté pan, heat the oil over medium. Add the onion and season with salt. Sauté until the onion begins to soften, about 3 minutes. Add the garlic and sauté until fragrant, about 1 minute. Add the cumin, coriander, and cayenne, and stir to coat the onion and garlic.

4. Add the quinoa, beans, tomato sauce, and lime juice. Stir to combine with the aromatics and spices and heat through, about 5 minutes. Season with salt. Remove from the heat and stir in the cilantro. (This makes about 4 cups.)

5. Remove the poblanos from the oven, place in a bowl, and cover with a plate or plastic wrap to trap in the heat. Set aside for 15 minutes. Reduce the oven temperature to 375°F. Grease a 13 × 9-inch baking dish with oil.

6. Once cooled, peel the skins off the poblanos. Leaving the stem intact, cut a pouch in the peeled poblano. Use a spoon to carefully remove the seeds.

7. Lay the poblanos side by side in the prepared baking dish. Stuff each pepper with one-sixth of the filling (about a heaping ½ cup). Top each with 2 tablespoons of the cheese.

8. Bake until the filling is completely warmed through and the cheese is melted and beginning to brown, 15 to 20 minutes.

9. Serve with fresh cilantro, avocado slices, and lime wedges.

NUTRITION, per serving

| Calories: 241 | Carbs: 33 grams | Fiber: 10 grams |
| Fat: 8 grams | Protein: 11 grams | Sugar: 4 grams |

shrimp ceviche and avocado tostadas

FOR 6 TOSTADAS

Traditional ceviche is a South American dish of raw seafood mixed in an acidic marinade such as citrus juice—the acid "cooks" the fish. This recipe uses cooked shrimp instead of raw fish. The fresh flavors of the cilantro, onion, cucumber, and tomato combined with the lemon and lime juices bring out the buttery sweetness of the shrimp. Plus, the crisp tostada gives the dish a wonderful crunch.

1 pound raw large shrimp, peeled, deveined, and tails removed

1 cup finely diced English cucumber

1 cup finely diced tomato

1 avocado, diced

1 cup finely diced red onion

Juice of 1 large lemon (about ¼ cup)

Juice of 1 large lime (about 2 tablespoons)

1 tablespoon roughly chopped fresh cilantro leaves

1 teaspoon kosher salt, plus more to taste

1 serrano pepper, finely chopped (optional)

6 corn tortillas

Extra-virgin olive oil

1. Roughly chop the shrimp (you should have about 3 cups) and transfer to a large bowl. Add the cucumber, tomato, avocado, onion, lemon and lime juices, cilantro, salt, and serrano (if using) and stir to combine. (This makes about 6 cups.) Marinate for about 1 hour in the refrigerator.

2. Preheat the oven to 425°F. Line a baking sheet with a reusable baking mat or parchment paper.

3. Lay the corn tortillas on the baking sheet and lightly brush both sides with oil.

4. Bake the tortillas for about 5 minutes and then flip them over. Continue baking until brown and crispy, about 5 minutes more. Set aside to cool.

5. Taste the ceviche for seasoning and add more salt if desired.

6. Spoon the shrimp mixture onto the cooled tostadas.

NUTRITION, per tostada

| Calories: 256 | Carbs: 23 grams | Fiber: 5 grams |
| Fat: 10 grams | Protein: 21 grams | Sugar: 4 grams |

roasted mushroom salad

VG GF

FOR 4 TO 6 SERVINGS

The crisped and caramelized roasted mushrooms are the star of this dish, bringing out a delicious umami flavor. Mushrooms contain B vitamins, which increase energy, and selenium, which strengthens immunity. With the additions of the peppery arugula and the honey mustard dressing, this salad will quickly become one of your go-tos.

MUSHROOMS

1 pound shiitake mushrooms, cleaned, stems removed, and halved

1 pound cremini mushrooms, cleaned, tough stems removed, and sliced

Extra-virgin olive oil

Kosher salt and freshly ground black pepper

2 garlic cloves, minced

1 small shallot, thinly sliced

1 cup frozen peas

⅓ cup roughly chopped fresh flat-leaf parsley

Zest of 1 unwaxed lemon (1 tablespoon)

5 ounces arugula (about 6 cups)

½ cup shaved Parmesan cheese, about 1¼ ounces

DRESSING (MAKES ABOUT ⅔ CUP)

2 teaspoons Dijon mustard

1 tablespoon raw honey

Juice of 1 lemon (about ¼ cup)

½ cup extra-virgin olive oil

Kosher salt

1. Preheat the oven to 425°F. Line two baking sheets with reusable baking mats or parchment paper.

2. Divide the mushrooms between the baking sheets and toss with oil, salt, and pepper. Roast until crispy and tender, 20 to 25 minutes.

3. Meanwhile, make the dressing. In a small bowl, whisk together the mustard, honey, and lemon juice. Slowly drizzle in the oil, whisking continuously until the dressing begins to thicken and emulsify. Season with salt.

4. After about 20 minutes, when the mushrooms are golden brown, remove them from the oven. Add the garlic, shallot, and peas to the mushrooms, season with salt and pepper, and stir to combine. Return to the oven and bake until the peas are warmed through and the shallot is soft, about 5 minutes more.

5. Remove the vegetables from the oven, sprinkle with the parsley and lemon zest, and set aside to cool slightly.

6. Put the arugula in a large bowl. Add the roasted vegetables to the arugula and toss with half of the dressing. Top with the shaved Parmesan and serve with the remaining dressing on the side. Any leftover dressing will keep in an airtight container in the refrigerator for up to 2 weeks.

NUTRITION, per serving

| Calories: 276 | Carbs: 20 grams | Fiber: 5 grams |
| Fat: 21 grams | Protein: 6 grams | Sugar: 9 grams |

lentil and walnut bolognese

FOR 8 SERVINGS

A big bowl of hearty pasta Bolognese is always satisfying and delicious. This version of the dish combines lentils and walnuts so that you can enjoy Bolognese without meat. The high-fiber lentils make the sauce filling and the walnuts add protein. Finished off with red wine, this Bolognese will feed your body and soul.

2 medium carrots, roughly chopped (about 1¼ cups)

3 celery stalks, roughly chopped (about 2 cups)

1 large white onion, roughly chopped (about 2 heaping cups)

3 garlic cloves, roughly chopped

1 cup roughly chopped raw walnuts

2 tablespoons extra-virgin olive oil

Kosher salt and freshly ground black pepper

2 teaspoons dried oregano

1 teaspoon dried basil

1 teaspoon dried parsley

2 tablespoons tomato paste

1 cup dry red wine

1 cup dried green lentils, sorted and rinsed well

2¾ cups low-sodium vegetable stock

1 (28-ounce) can petite diced tomatoes

Pasta of choice, prepared according to package directions

1. In a food processor, pulse the carrots, celery, onion, and garlic until finely chopped but not mushy. Remove from the food processor bowl and scrape the bowl clean.

2. Pulse the walnuts until minced. Set aside.

3. Heat a large pot over medium-high and add the oil. Add the vegetable mixture and season with salt, the oregano, basil, and parsley. Cook until the mixture has caramelized and the excess moisture has evaporated, stirring throughout to avoid burning, about 20 minutes.

4. Mix in the tomato paste and cook, stirring constantly, until slightly deepened in color, 3 to 5 minutes. Add the wine and stir, scraping up any bits from the bottom of the pan. Cook until the sauce is almost completely reduced, about 3 minutes.

5. Add the lentils, walnuts, stock, and tomatoes and season with salt. Lower the heat to medium, cover, and simmer, stirring occasionally, until the lentils are cooked through and the walnuts are softened, 30 to 35 minutes.

6. Remove the lid and cook off any remaining liquid, stirring frequently, about 5 minutes.

7. Taste for seasoning and add salt and pepper if needed. Serve over pasta.

NUTRITION, per serving

| Calories: 262 | Carbs: 18 grams | Fiber: 6 grams |
| Fat: 16 grams | Protein: 7 grams | Sugar: 5 grams |

kimchi
fried rice

FOR 2 SERVINGS

Kimchi has an addictive, effervescent quality thanks to the fermentation process that the cabbage (and sometimes radish) undergoes to create this signature Korean dish. The fermentation process imparts healthy bacteria called lactobacilli, which help with digestion. Gochujang is a sweet-and-spicy red chili paste; if you can't find it at your local supermarket, you can order it online, and it'll keep in the refrigerator for up to two years. This dish comes together in under 30 minutes and is packed with amazing flavors.

FRIED RICE

1 tablespoon sesame or avocado oil

1 small yellow onion, finely diced

1 garlic clove, minced

1 inch fresh ginger, peeled and minced

Kosher salt

½ cup kimchi, roughly chopped, with its liquid

3 cups cooked brown rice

½ cup frozen peas and carrots, thawed

2 tablespoons soy sauce (or tamari if gluten-free)

1 tablespoon gochujang paste

1 teaspoon toasted sesame oil

GARNISHES

2 scallions, light green parts only, thinly sliced lengthwise

1 tablespoon roasted sesame seeds

1 sheet nori, sliced into strips

2 free-range eggs, fried (optional)

1. In a wok or large sauté pan, heat the oil over medium-high to high.

2. When the oil is shimmering and almost smoking, add the onion and cook until soft and just beginning to brown, 5 to 6 minutes. Add the garlic and ginger and cook until fragrant, about 1 minute. Season with salt. Add the chopped kimchi and its liquid and stir until heated through, 1 to 2 minutes. Add the rice and peas and carrots, and stir to combine.

3. Add the soy sauce, gochujang, and toasted sesame oil, and stir until the rice is well coated. Spread the rice into an even layer and cook, undisturbed, until a light crust develops, 2 to 3 minutes. Season with salt.

4. Divide between two plates and top with the scallions, sesame seeds, nori, and fried eggs, if desired.

NUTRITION, per serving (with egg)

Calories: 611	Carbs: 89 grams	Fiber: 9 grams
Fat: 21 grams	Protein: 18 grams	Sugar: 8 grams

immunity-supporting green soup

DF

Yes, green juice is all the rage, but have you tried green soup? Eating a lot of greens can sometimes be a challenge, but this soup makes it easy and delicious. Swiss chard, spinach, and broccoli are rich sources of vitamin C, a well-known immunity booster. Turmeric and ginger also do wonders for the immune system. Blend these all together with a creamy avocado and you have a warming, savory soup.

2 tablespoons extra-virgin olive oil

8 garlic cloves, minced

4 scallions, chopped

3 inches fresh ginger, peeled and sliced

3 tablespoons fresh oregano leaves

1 cup freshly chopped flat-leaf parsley, plus more for garnish

¼ teaspoon cayenne pepper

1 teaspoon ground turmeric

½ teaspoon freshly ground black pepper

2 tablespoons low-sodium soy sauce

4 cups broccoli florets, tough stems trimmed

6 cups low-sodium chicken or vegetable stock (see page 237 for a homemade version)

4 cups roughly chopped Swiss chard leaves

1 pound baby spinach

1 large ripe avocado, diced

Juice of 1 large lemon (about ¼ cup)

Kosher salt

Toasted pepitas (pumpkin seeds), for garnish (optional)

1. Heat the oil in a large pot over medium heat. Add the garlic, scallions, and ginger. Sauté the aromatics until very fragrant but not browned, about 3 minutes.

2. Add the oregano, parsley, cayenne, turmeric, black pepper, and soy sauce. Cook until the herbs begin to wilt, about 2 minutes.

3. Add the broccoli florets and cook until they are bright green and beginning to release some moisture, about 5 minutes.

4. Add the stock. Cover and bring to a low simmer. Cook until the broccoli starts to soften, about 10 minutes after covering. (If you cook the broccoli for 10 minutes after bringing it to simmer, it will get too soft.)

5. Remove the lid, add the chard, and stir until wilted, about 30 seconds. Add the baby spinach a few handfuls at a time. Cook until just wilted, stirring to incorporate the leaves into the soup before adding more. Remove the soup from the heat when the greens are wilted and the broccoli stems can be easily pierced with a fork. It is important not to overcook the greens, as they will begin to lose their vibrant color and nutrients.

6. Using an immersion blender, purée the soup briefly to combine. If using a high-speed blender, cool the soup until it can be safely transferred, about 15 minutes. If your blender is not big enough to blend the soup all at once, blend the soup in separate batches. Remove the small cap from the lid of the blender, then cover the opening with a kitchen towel. This will help to release excess steam while blending.

7. Add the avocado and lemon juice, season with salt, and blend again until creamy and no lumps remain.

8. Enjoy the soup hot or cold, garnished with more parsley and toasted pepitas, if desired.

NUTRITION, per serving

| Calories: 189 | Carbs: 21 grams | Fiber: 7 grams |
| Fat: 9 grams | Protein: 10 grams | Sugar: 5 grams |

coconut broth clams

FOR 4 SERVINGS

We know that clams can be a polarizing ingredient and intimidating to make at home. Don't fear! These are delicious and we'll walk you through it step by step. Clams are one of the most potent food sources of zinc, and they're also high in iron. The lemongrass, often used in Southeast Asian recipes, is heavenly with the coconut milk, and you can even save the stems to make a tea.

CLAMS

2 pounds littleneck clams or 1½ pounds Manila clams (14 to 20 clams), scrubbed

Cold water, for soaking

Sea salt

GRILLED BREAD

1 sourdough baguette, about 12 ounces

2 tablespoons extra-virgin olive oil, for brushing

Sea salt

COCONUT BROTH

1 tablespoon unrefined coconut oil

½ medium red onion, thinly sliced

2 large lemongrass stalks

3 tablespoons minced fresh ginger (about 2 inches)

4 or 5 garlic cloves, minced

1 teaspoon crushed red pepper flakes, or 2 Thai chili peppers, minced

1 cup dry white wine

1 tablespoon light brown sugar

1 tablespoon fish sauce or low-sodium soy sauce

2 cups vegetable or chicken stock

1 (13-ounce) can full-fat unsweetened coconut milk, shaken thoroughly before opening

GARNISHES

Thinly sliced scallions

Fresh chopped cilantro

1. Pick through the clams and discard any that are open and do not close when firmly tapped—these clams are dead and should not be eaten. Add the rest to a colander.

2. Rinse and scrub the clams to remove any sand or barnacles from the shells. Fill a bowl large enough to fit the colander with cold water and 3 to 4 tablespoons salt for every 6 cups water. Stir until most of the salt has dissolved. Place the colander in the bowl of salt water and soak the clams for at least 1 hour and up to overnight, so they release any grit and sand. (Live clams will filter the water and push out any impurities in the process; the grit falls to the bottom of the bowl and the colander allows you to lift out the clams without disturbing the grit.)

3. Transfer the clams in the colander to another large bowl of fresh water and let soak for 15 to 30 minutes to remove excess salt.

4. Meanwhile, slice the sourdough baguette into ½-inch-thick pieces, about 32 pieces total. Brush each slice with olive oil and sprinkle with salt.

5. Toast the bread on a grill pan over medium-high heat until golden brown and crusty, about 2 minutes per side. Set aside.

6. In a wok or large pan, melt the coconut oil over medium heat. Add the onion and cook until translucent, 3 to 4 minutes.

7. Firmly whack the lemongrass stalks with a wooden spoon to bruise them, which helps release their aroma and flavor during cooking. Trim the ends, then slice the stalks into 4-inch pieces. Add the lemongrass to the wok, then add the ginger, garlic, and red pepper flakes. Cook until fragrant, about 3 minutes.

8. Carefully pour in the white wine and stir to deglaze the pan. Bring to a simmer and cook until reduced by half, about 5 minutes.

9. Add the brown sugar, fish sauce, stock, and coconut milk and bring to a boil. Add the clams, return to a boil, and cook until the clams are fully opened, 5 to 8 minutes. If any clams remain closed, discard them. Discard the lemongrass.

10. Divide the clams and broth among individual serving bowls. Garnish with scallions and cilantro and serve with the grilled bread for dipping in the broth.

NUTRITION, per serving

| Calories: 434 | Carbs: 17 grams | Fiber: 0 grams |
| Fat: 26 grams | Protein: 25 grams | Sugar: 5 grams |

cider-braised pork chops

FOR 2 SERVINGS

These pork chops are especially tender thanks to brining, which is the process of placing a cut of meat in a water-and-salt solution. The meat absorbs the seasoned liquid, making it juicier and more flavorful. This technique is ideal for lean cuts of meat that tend to dry out during cooking. Dijon mustard and apple cider round out the flavors in this dish, and collard greens are the perfect pairing to make it a complete meal.

BRINE

4 cups water

2 bay leaves

4 garlic cloves, crushed

1 tablespoon black peppercorns

⅓ cup fine sea salt

4 cups ice

PORK CHOPS

2 (1-inch-thick) bone-in pork chops, about 2 pounds

Fine sea salt and freshly ground black pepper

1 tablespoon high-heat cooking oil of choice, such as vegetable or peanut

2 medium shallots, diced

3 cups diced turnips

1 tablespoon Dijon mustard

1 tablespoon freshly chopped sage

2 cups apple cider

1 cup low-sodium chicken stock

1 bunch collard greens, leaves stemmed and roughly chopped (about 4 cups packed)

1. In a medium pot over medium heat, combine the water, bay leaves, garlic, peppercorns, and salt. Stir until the salt is dissolved, about 3 minutes.

2. Remove the brine from the heat and stir in the ice cubes. Once the brine is cooled, put the pork chops in a glass dish and pour the brine over them. Brine in the refrigerator for at least 1 hour and up to 10 hours.

3. Preheat the oven to 350°F.

4. Remove the pork chops from the brine and pat dry. Season lightly with salt and pepper on both sides.

5. Heat the oil in a large cast-iron or other ovenproof skillet over medium-high until nearly smoking. Add the pork chops and sear without moving them, until caramelized and browned on the first side, 2 to 4 minutes, then flip and sear on the other side for 2 to 4 minutes more. Remove the pork chops from the pan and set aside.

6. Add the shallots to the pan and cook, stirring constantly, until they begin to soften and caramelize, 1 to 2 minutes.

7. Add the turnips and season with salt, and then spread in an even layer and cook, stirring occasionally, until caramelized, about 5 minutes. Stir in the mustard and sage. Cook until the sage is fragrant, about 1 minute more.

8. Pour in the apple cider and chicken stock. Bring to a boil, then reduce the heat to medium-low and simmer until the liquid is reduced by half, 7 to 10 minutes.

9. Add the collard greens and stir to incorporate. Nestle the pork chops into the sauce, making sure they are partly submerged.

10. Transfer the pan to the oven and cook until the internal temperature of the pork chops reaches 135°F, 12 to 18 minutes.

11. Remove from the oven and let rest for about 10 minutes as the internal temperature continues to climb to 145°F.

12. Divide the pork chops, vegetables, and sauce between two plates and serve.

NUTRITION, per serving

| Calories: 490 | Carbs: 53 grams | Fiber: 7 grams |
| Fat: 27 grams | Protein: 48 grams | Sugar: 10 grams |

lemon tahini veggie flatbread

FOR 4 SERVINGS

Creamy tahini has a delicate roasted sesame flavor that is the perfect balance for the caramelized roasted cauliflower and onions that top this flatbread. Tahini is made from ground sesame seeds, which are a good source of amino acids, vitamin E, B vitamins, and fatty acids—all great for your skin. This recipe makes an easy homemade flatbread, but store-bought flatbread works too. Finished with briny olives, mint, and parsley, this fresh vegan meal will not disappoint.

FLATBREAD

1½ teaspoons organic sugar

2¼ teaspoons active dry yeast (one ¼-ounce packet)

¼ cup warm water

2 cups white whole-wheat flour

2 teaspoons kosher salt

1 tablespoon extra-virgin olive oil

½ to 1 cup cold water

VEGGIES

1 teaspoon cumin

1 teaspoon dried oregano

1 teaspoon dried thyme

½ teaspoon paprika

5 cups cauliflower florets, about 1 pound (roughly 1 small head)

1 medium red onion, thinly sliced

2 tablespoons extra-virgin olive oil

Kosher salt

TAHINI SPREAD (MAKES ABOUT ½ CUP)

¼ cup tahini, about 2½ ounces, well stirred

2 garlic cloves, minced

Zest and juice of ½ large unwaxed lemon (½ teaspoon zest and 2 tablespoons juice)

Kosher salt and freshly ground black pepper

TOPPINGS

½ cup pitted briny green olives, such as Castelvetrano olives, halved

Tahini, well stirred

¼ cup fresh mint leaves

¼ cup freshly chopped flat-leaf parsley leaves

1. Preheat the oven to 400°F. Lightly oil a large bowl.

2. In a small bowl, combine the sugar, yeast, and warm water. Set aside for about 10 minutes to bloom.

3. In a large bowl, combine the flour and salt. After the yeast mixture blooms, pour the yeast mixture and the oil into the flour. Mix in the cold water in ¼-cup increments until a dough forms. Transfer the dough to a floured surface and knead until the dough is smooth and springs back when you press into it with your finger, about 5 minutes. Place the dough in the oiled bowl, cover with plastic wrap, and set aside in a warm area to rise until almost doubled in size, 30 minutes to 1 hour.

4. While the dough rises, mix together the cumin, oregano, thyme, and paprika. Put the cauliflower on half of a large unlined baking sheet and put the onion on the other half. Drizzle the cauliflower and onion with the oil, then sprinkle with half of the spice mixture and season generously with salt. Toss the vegetables to coat, being careful to keep them separate.

5. Roast until the cauliflower is nicely browned in spots and fork-tender, about 20 minutes. Stir the onion halfway through, leaving the cauliflower undisturbed. Remove from the oven, sprinkle with the remaining spice mixture, then stir the vegetables gently until combined. Set aside.

6. Increase the oven temperature to 500°F.

7. In a medium bowl, whisk together the tahini, garlic, and lemon zest and juice. Add enough cold water to achieve a consistency that is spreadable and smooth. Season well with salt and pepper.

8. Turn the dough out onto a floured surface and cut it into four pieces. Roll each piece out to an oblong or rough rectangle shape about ⅛ inch thick.

9. Oil a baking sheet. Transfer the flatbreads to the baking sheet (you may need to use two sheets or to work in batches). Bake until the bottom is golden brown and crispy and the top has some bubbles and is mostly golden brown, 8 to 12 minutes. Remove the flatbreads from the oven.

10. To assemble, spread 1 to 2 tablespoons of the tahini spread onto each flatbread, then top with the roasted vegetables and olives. Drizzle with plain tahini and sprinkle with the fresh herbs. Enjoy warm or cold.

NUTRITION, per serving

| Calories: 491 | Carbs: 72 grams | Fiber: 16 grams |
| Fat: 18 grams | Protein: 19 grams | Sugar: 8 grams |

tableside hot pot

FOR 4 SERVINGS

The perfect communal meal for a unique gathering with family or friends, the hot pot is a Chinese tabletop cooking method in which you cook ingredients by placing them in a simmering pot of soup stock. This recipe is special because it's totally customizable. Each person can pick and choose which ingredients to add to the pot and cook them as rare or well-done as they like. Feel free to add your favorite veggie and sauces. The options are limitless!

BROTH

8 cups low-sodium beef, chicken, or vegetable stock (64 ounces)

4 garlic cloves, peeled and halved

2 inches fresh ginger, halved

1 yellow onion, quartered

¼ cup Shaoxing wine (Chinese cooking wine) or dry sherry

1½ teaspoons Szechuan peppercorns

3 bay leaves

1 star anise

¼ cup low-sodium soy sauce

TABLESIDE SUGGESTIONS (PICK YOUR FAVORITES!)

Proteins

Thinly shaved beef, lamb, pork, and/or chicken (many Asian markets will sell meat perfectly sliced for hot pot)

Raw shrimp, deveined

Firm tofu, sliced

Vegetables

Shiitake mushrooms, stemmed and thinly sliced

Baby bok choy

Chinese broccoli

Lotus flower root, sliced

Napa cabbage, shredded

Baby corn

Green beans

Snow peas

Japanese or Chinese eggplant, thinly sliced

Other

Frozen dumplings

Fresh noodles

For Garnish

4 scallions, thinly sliced

¼ cup white sesame seeds

2 cups cooked brown rice

Low-sodium soy sauce

Chili oil

1. In a large Dutch oven or hotpot pot over medium-high heat, place the stock, garlic, ginger, onion, wine, peppercorns, bay leaves, star anise, and soy sauce. Bring to a simmer and cook until fragrant, about 1 hour. Strain the broth and compost or discard the solids.

2. Place a hot plate or camping stove on a table. Return the strained broth to the Dutch oven, set it on the hot plate, and heat it to a bare simmer.

3. Serve the accompaniments on platters separated by the cook time and type of food for guests to customize their meal. For instance, mushrooms and other vegetables with thick stems need to simmer for a few minutes, while thinly sliced beef needs only about 30 seconds in the broth.

4. Have tongs or long chopsticks on each platter to be used as communal cooking utensils so guests can reserve their personal chopsticks for eating. Give each guest a bowl with ½ cup of rice to place their cooked food onto, as well as a small dish filled with soy sauce.

5. As you cook the meat and vegetables, the broth will become more and more flavorful. It's customary to end the meal with fresh noodles cooked in the flavorful broth. If you have both vegetarians and meat eaters at the table, we recommend separating the broth into two pots to keep one vegetarian.

NUTRITION, per serving of broth only

| Calories: 66 | Carbs: 10 grams | Fiber: 0 grams |
| Fat: 0 grams | Protein: 3 grams | Sugar: 3 grams |

wine-braised beef

FOR 5 SERVINGS (SAUCE MAKES ABOUT 2 CUPS;
BEEF MAKES ABOUT 3⅓ CUPS)

This beef is so tender that it falls apart and melts in your mouth. The wine and caramelized vegetables enhance the rich flavors, making this dish something that will warm you from the inside out. We recommend serving this with cauliflower mash, pasta, brown rice, or roasted vegetables. *Bon appétit!*

2 pounds sustainably raised grass-fed beef chuck roast, cut into 1-inch pieces

Kosher salt and freshly ground black pepper

4 tablespoons extra-virgin olive oil

1½ cups dry red wine, such as Malbec, Zinfandel, or Cabernet Sauvignon

2 yellow onions, quartered

3 large carrots, cut into 1-inch pieces

3 celery stalks, about 6 ounces, cut into 1-inch pieces

1 fennel bulb, quartered, fronds saved for garnish

6 garlic cloves, peeled

¼ cup tomato paste

2 sprigs oregano, plus more for garnish

2 sprigs marjoram, plus more for garnish

2 bay leaves

2 cups low-sodium beef stock or water, as needed

1. Preheat the oven to 300°F.

2. Season the beef with salt and pepper on all sides. In a large Dutch oven over medium-high heat, add 2 tablespoons of the oil. Heat until nearly smoking, then add the beef. Working in batches, sear the meat on all sides, 6 to 7 minutes total, turning as needed. Once brown, place the beef in a large bowl. Repeat with the remaining beef. If at any point it appears the pan is getting too hot or scorching, quickly cool it down by adding a splash of the wine. Once all the beef is seared, deglaze the pan with a splash of wine and carefully pour the juices into the bowl with the beef.

3. Add 1 tablespoon of the oil to the pan. Once the oil is hot, add an even layer of the onions, carrots, celery, fennel, and garlic and sear in batches. Season each batch with salt and pepper. Once the vegetables have softened and are deeply browned and caramelized, transfer them to the bowl with the beef. Use the remaining 1 tablespoon oil as needed while searing the remaining vegetables. Once all the vegetables have been cooked and removed from the pan, add the tomato paste to the pan and stir continuously until it's toasted and turns a deep dark red, about 2 minutes. Pour in a splash of the wine and deglaze the pan, stirring to combine the paste and wine.

4. Place the beef and vegetables back in the Dutch oven and pour in any juices from the bowl, then add the remaining wine. Add the oregano, marjoram, and bay leaves. If the wine does not cover the beef and vegetables, add the stock as needed, up to 2 cups. Bring to a boil and cover with a lid.

5. Place the pot in the oven and bake until the beef is fork-tender but still holds its shape, 3 to 3½ hours.

6. Remove from the oven and transfer the beef to a plate. Strain the cooking juices, pressing the vegetables to get all the juice through the sieve. Compost or discard the solids.

7. Return the juices to the pot, skimming off any excess fat on top. Bring the liquid to a simmer and cook until reduced by a third to about 2 cups, about 10 minutes. Taste for seasoning and add salt and pepper, if needed. Return the beef to the sauce.

8. Roughly chop the fennel fronds, oregano, and marjoram leaves together. Serve the braised beef with the chopped herbs on top.

NUTRITION, per serving

| Calories: 643 | Carbs: 25 grams | Fiber: 6 grams |
| Fat: 33 grams | Protein: 42 grams | Sugar: 11 grams |

linguine and clams

FOR 2 SERVINGS

You're going to want to keep this classic recipe in your back pocket. Clams are super sustainable, inexpensive, and nutrient-dense. Loaded with iron and protein, they're good for building and maintaining muscle—and while they may seem intimidating, they are incredibly easy to prepare.

1 pound littleneck clams or Manila clams, scrubbed (7 to 10 clams)

6 cups cold water, for soaking (about 1½ liters)

3 tablespoons sea salt

Kosher salt

½ pound uncooked brown rice linguine or pasta of choice

¼ cup extra-virgin olive oil

2 garlic cloves, thinly sliced

¼ teaspoon crushed red pepper flakes

3 Roma or vine-ripened tomatoes, cored, seeded, and finely diced

⅓ cup dry white wine, such as Pinot Grigio

Zest and juice of 1 unwaxed lemon (about 1 tablespoon zest and ¼ cup juice)

¼ cup roughly chopped fresh flat-leaf parsley

¼ cup shredded Parmesan cheese (optional)

Freshly ground black pepper (optional)

1. Pick through the clams and discard any that are open and do not close when firmly tapped—these clams are dead and should not be eaten. Add the rest to a colander.

2. Rinse and scrub the clams to remove any sand or barnacles from the shells. Fill a bowl large enough to fit the colander with 6 cups cold water and add the salt. Place the colander in the bowl of salt water and soak the clams for at least 1 hour and up to overnight, so they release any grit and sand. (Live clams will filter the water and push out any impurities in the process; the grit falls to the bottom of the bowl and the colander allows you to lift out the clams without disturbing the grit.)

3. Transfer the clams in the colander to another large bowl of fresh water and let soak for 15 to 30 minutes to remove excess salt.

4. Fill a large pot of water, generously season with salt, and bring to a boil. Cook the pasta for 2 minutes shy of package directions. Reserve ½ cup of the cooking water, then drain.

5. Heat a tall saucepan over medium. Add the oil and heat until shimmering. Add the garlic, red pepper flakes, and tomatoes. Season with a pinch of salt. Cook, stirring frequently, for about 3 minutes. Deglaze with the wine.

6. Quickly add the clams to the saucepan and cover with a tight-fitting lid. Cook, shaking the pan occasionally, until the clams open, 5 to 8 minutes. Discard any clams that did not open during cooking.

7. Add the pasta, lemon zest and juice, parsley, a splash of the pasta cooking water, and the Parmesan (if using). Stir to combine. Taste for seasoning and add salt and pepper, if needed.

NUTRITION, per serving

| Calories: 616 | Carbs: 48 grams | Fiber: 5 grams |
| Fat: 32 grams | Protein: 27 grams | Sugar: 6 grams |

miso butter–seared sea bass
with roasted vegetables

FOR 2 SERVINGS

This recipe makes miso happy and we hope it makes you happy too! White miso, also known as sweet or mellow miso, is made from soybeans that have been fermented with rice, and it is lower in salt than darker versions. It's tasty in soups, dressings, and sauces, and is used instead of dairy in vegan recipes like miso mashed potatoes. This under-30-minute preparation pairs well with heart-healthy sea bass and really boosts the flavors of the veggies.

2 tablespoons unsalted grass-fed butter, softened

3 tablespoons gluten-free mellow white miso

1 tablespoon grated fresh ginger

3 garlic cloves, grated

1 teaspoon toasted sesame oil

½ pound baby potatoes, halved (about 1½ cups)

3 tablespoons sunflower oil or cooking oil of choice

Kosher salt and freshly ground black pepper

2 (1- to 1¼-inch-thick) pieces Chilean sea bass, skin on, 4 to 6 ounces each

2 baby bok choy, thinly sliced

1 teaspoon white sesame seeds, toasted if desired

1. Preheat the oven to 400°F. Line a baking sheet with a reusable baking mat or parchment paper.

2. In a small bowl, stir together the butter, miso, ginger, garlic, and sesame oil and set aside.

3. Arrange the potatoes on the baking sheet, drizzle with ½ tablespoon of the sunflower oil, and season with salt and pepper. Roast until tender, 8 to 12 minutes.

4. While the potatoes roast, sear the sea bass. Pat each fillet dry with a clean kitchen towel or paper towel and season with salt and pepper on all sides, including the skin side.

5. In a medium skillet over medium-high heat, add 2 tablespoons of the sunflower oil. Once the oil is shimmering and nearly smoking, add the bass, skin-side down, and cook until the skin is crispy, 3 to 4 minutes. Flip and sear the second side until golden brown, about 3 minutes. Remove from the heat.

6. Remove the potatoes from the oven and make room for the fillets and bok choy on the pan. Add 1 teaspoon of the miso butter to the flesh side of each fillet and add the fillets to the pan, skin-side up. Add 1 more teaspoon of miso butter to the skin side of each fillet. Add the bok choy to the pan, then season with the remaining ½ tablespoon sunflower oil and salt and pepper to taste.

7. Return the baking sheet to the oven and bake until the fish is completely opaque and just cooked through, 8 to 10 minutes. The internal temperature of the sea bass should read 130°F.

8. Garnish with the sesame seeds and serve immediately.

NUTRITION per serving

Calories: 480	Carbs: 37 grams	Fiber: 6 grams
Fat: 25 grams	Protein: 29 grams	Sugar: 5 grams

flank steak

with chimichurri and roasted purple potatoes

FOR 4 SERVINGS

We love chimichurri sauce for its bold, fresh flavor and vibrant green color. This South American specialty is a garlicky uncooked sauce commonly served with grilled meat. Chimichurri is the perfect kick for this succulent flank steak. The purple potatoes are higher in antioxidants than other types of potatoes and they add a fun pop of color to the plate. When making the sauce, compost the parsley stems or save them for making stock.

CHIMICHURRI (MAKES ABOUT 1 CUP)

Leaves from 1 bunch flat-leaf parsley (1½ cups packed)

10 basil leaves

Leaves from 2 sprigs oregano

2 garlic cloves, smashed and peeled

1 to 1½ teaspoons crushed red pepper flakes

1 teaspoon smoked paprika

1 bay leaf, finely ground

¼ cup red wine vinegar

½ cup extra-virgin olive oil

STEAK AND POTATOES

2 pounds flank steak

Kosher salt and freshly ground black pepper

1 pound purple fingerling potatoes (about 14), cut into ½-inch cubes (about 3½ cups)

2 tablespoons avocado oil or cooking oil of choice, plus more for searing the steak

1. Make the chimichurri by hand or with a food processor. If using a food processor, place the herbs, smashed garlic cloves, red pepper flakes, paprika, and bay leaf into the bowl of the processor. Pulse about 15 times, until finely chopped. Add the vinegar and olive oil and run the processor until a fine paste forms. If making by hand, finely chop the herbs and garlic and put them in a medium bowl along with the rest of the chimichurri ingredients. Stir to combine. Place in the refrigerator for about 1 hour to marinate.

2. Pat the steak dry with a clean kitchen towel or paper towels. Place on a platter or large plate and season on both sides with salt and pepper. Refrigerate, uncovered, for about 1 hour.

3. In a medium saucepan, cover the potatoes by 1 inch with cold water and generously salt the water. Bring to a boil and cook until the potatoes are tender but still hold their shape, about 10 minutes.

4. While the potatoes are cooking, preheat the oven to 450°F. Pour 2 tablespoons of avocado oil into a baking sheet and preheat in the oven for about 5 minutes prior to roasting the potatoes.

5. Drain the potatoes, put them back in the pot, and allow to steam dry for about 3 minutes. Carefully add the potatoes to the preheated baking sheet, making sure to pour the potatoes away from you onto the pan so the oil doesn't splash back, then shake the pan gently to ensure the potatoes are evenly coated with the hot oil. Roast until deeply golden brown and crispy, 20 to 25 minutes.

RECIPE CONTINUES

6. Heat a large cast-iron skillet over medium-high. Add the avocado oil and heat until shimmering and almost smoking. Sear the steak without disturbing it until deeply caramelized, about 6 minutes. Flip and sear for about 5 minutes more for medium-rare. The steak should be caramelized on the second side and register 130°F on an instant meat thermometer. For a medium or well-done steak, flip once more and transfer to the hot oven; cook for 5 to 10 minutes, depending on your desired doneness.

7. Rest the steak for about 10 minutes before slicing. Season the potatoes with salt and pepper. Serve with the chimichurri. Any leftover steak and chimichurri goes great with eggs in the morning. The sauce will last in an airtight container in the refrigerator for up to 1 week, although it will start to lose its bright-green color.

NUTRITION, per serving of steak and potatoes

| Calories: 663 | Carbs: 24 grams | Fiber: 3 grams |
| Fat: 32 grams | Protein: 66 grams | Sugar: 1 gram |

NUTRITION, per 2 tablespoons chimichurri

| Calories: 126 | Carbs: 1 gram | Fiber: 0 grams |
| Fat: 14 grams | Protein: 0 grams | Sugar: 0 grams |

two-pan balsamic chicken legs
with delicata squash and leeks

FOR 3 OR 4 SERVINGS

Why not try out some new veggies with this delicious dinner option? Delicata is a squash that tastes like butternut but with a richer flavor and softer skin. It's also easier to prep, and really just beautiful. Leeks have a sweet, mild onion flavor, and they offer many of the same health benefits as garlic and onions.

4 leeks

2 delicata squash, or 1 acorn squash, about 1 pound 6 ounces

4 skin-on chicken leg quarters (leg and thigh), about 2 pounds total

4 garlic cloves, smashed but not peeled

4 sprigs rosemary

2 teaspoons kosher salt

1 teaspoon freshly ground black pepper

2 tablespoons avocado oil

¼ cup balsamic vinegar

1. Preheat the oven to 400°F. Line two baking sheets with reusable baking mats or parchment paper.

2. Cut the top third off each of the leeks, where the light green starts to become dark green, and compost, discard, or freeze the dark green section for next time you're making vegetable stock. Slice each leek in half lengthwise and remove the outer two layers. Wash the leeks under cold running water to remove any sand or dirt.

3. Remove the root and stem ends from each squash and cut in half. Scoop out the seeds and compost. If using delicata, slice the halves into ¼-inch-thick half-moons. If using acorn, cut the two halves in half lengthwise and then cut into ¼-inch-wide wedges. Add the vegetables in an even layer to one baking sheet. Add any remaining squash to the second baking sheet.

4. Place the chicken on the second baking sheet. Divide the garlic and rosemary between the sheets. Season each baking sheet with half the salt, pepper, oil, and balsamic vinegar. Toss to combine and then spread the chicken and vegetables out in an even layer.

5. Roast until the vegetables and chicken are golden brown, the vinegar has reduced to a syrup, and the chicken has an internal temperature of 165°F, about 40 minutes, turning the chicken and vegetables halfway through.

6. When cool enough to handle, peel the garlic and mash it into a paste. Toss the garlic with the squash and serve the chicken, squash, and leeks on a platter. Garnish with the crispy rosemary sprigs.

NUTRITION, per serving

| Calories: 635 | Carbs: 23 grams | Fiber: 5 grams |
| Fat: 31 grams | Protein: 64 grams | Sugar: 8 grams |

chicken breasts in peanut sauce

(DF)

FOR 4 SERVINGS

With hints of ginger, lemongrass, and red curry, this is the kind of sauce you want to eat with a spoon. Between the broccoli and red bell peppers, there are lots of veggies. Your local delivery restaurant will be missing you tonight!

½ teaspoon freshly ground black pepper, plus more to taste

3 boneless, skinless chicken breasts

1 teaspoon kosher salt, plus more to taste

1 tablespoon avocado oil, plus more as needed

1 medium yellow onion, thinly sliced

1 medium carrot, thinly sliced on the bias

2 garlic cloves, minced

1 inch fresh ginger, grated

1 jalapeño, seeded and diced

1 lemongrass stalk, halved and bruised with the back of a spoon

¼ cup Thai red curry paste

⅓ cup creamy all-natural peanut butter

¼ cup low-sodium soy sauce

2 tablespoons fish sauce

1½ cups pure coconut water

1 red bell pepper, seeded and thinly sliced

2 cups bite-size broccoli florets

Zest and juice of 3 limes (about ⅓ cup of juice)

¼ cup roughly chopped fresh cilantro

¼ cup chopped roasted salted peanuts

Cooked rice noodles, cauliflower rice, or toasted flatbread, for serving

1. Place a large Dutch oven over medium-high heat. Add the oil to the pot and heat until shimmering.

2. Cut the chicken into 1-inch pieces and season with the salt and pepper. Add half the chicken to the Dutch oven in an even layer and cook until golden brown on all sides, flipping as needed, 8 to 10 minutes. Transfer the chicken to a clean bowl, add another tablespoon of oil as needed, and repeat with the remaining chicken. Set aside.

3. Add the onion, carrot, garlic, ginger, jalapeño, and lemongrass to the pot. Season with salt and pepper, stir, and cook until the vegetables have softened and are just beginning to brown, 3 to 4 minutes. Push the vegetables to the side of the pan and add the curry paste and peanut butter, without touching the vegetables. Stir to combine the curry paste with the peanut butter and toast for 1 minute, then stir the vegetables and the peanut butter mixture together.

4. Add the soy sauce, fish sauce, coconut water, bell pepper, and broccoli and stir to combine. Return the chicken to the pan and stir. Bring to a simmer, cover, and cook until the chicken is cooked through, about 10 minutes.

5. Remove the lemongrass. Add the lime zest and juice and season with salt and pepper. Top with the cilantro and crushed peanuts and serve over rice noodles.

NUTRITION, per serving

Calories: 663	Carbs: 35 grams	Fiber: 9 grams
Fat: 26 grams	Protein: 74 grams	Sugar: 11 grams

low-carb pad thai

FOR 4 SERVINGS

What's more crave-worthy than the tangle of sweet, sour, nutty, and spicy noodles known as pad thai? The traditional take-out version is heavy on the simple carbs and low on the veggies, but our version preserves the flavor while swapping the rice noodles for zucchini noodles.

2 small zucchini

1 medium sweet potato, peeled

1 (6-inch) daikon radish, peeled

2 tablespoons dark brown sugar

2 tablespoons fish sauce

2 tablespoons tamarind paste or freshly squeezed lime juice

6 garlic cloves, minced

¼ cup water

1 tablespoon refined coconut oil, plus more if needed

1 pound boneless, skinless chicken thighs, sliced

Kosher salt

1 medium shallot, thinly sliced

2 teaspoons chili paste, or 1 jalapeño, diced

⅓ cup roasted peanuts, plus more for garnish

½ cup bean sprouts, plus more for garnish

¼ cup fresh cilantro leaves, plus more for garnish

Lime wedges, for garnish

1. Trim the ends of the zucchini, then use a vegetable peeler to cut the zucchini into thin, flat noodles, stopping once you get to the seedy core, making about 2 cups total. Compost or discard the core. Repeat with the sweet potato and daikon radish, making about 1 cup of each. Set aside.

2. In a wok or large pan over medium-high heat, combine the brown sugar, fish sauce, tamarind paste, half the garlic, and the water. Cook until the sugar has dissolved and the sauce is slightly thickened, 2 to 3 minutes.

3. Remove the pan from the heat and transfer the pad Thai sauce to a bowl until ready to use. Wipe out the pan or give it a quick rinse, if needed.

4. Melt the coconut oil in the same pan over medium-high heat. Lightly season the chicken thighs with salt, then add to the pan and sear until browned and cooked through, 3 to 4 minutes per side. Remove the chicken from the pan and set aside.

5. Add a bit more coconut oil to the pan, if needed, then add the shallot, chili paste, and the remaining garlic. Cook until the shallot is softened and the aromatics are fragrant, about 2 minutes.

6. Add the peanuts and bean sprouts, and cook until the sprouts are softened, about 1 minute. Add the pad thai sauce and stir to combine.

7. Add the vegetable noodles and chicken, and stir to coat with the sauce. Cook until the noodles are just warmed through but not soggy, about 2 minutes. Turn off the heat and stir in the cilantro.

8. Serve immediately, garnished with more cilantro, bean sprouts, peanuts, and lime wedges.

NUTRITION, per serving

Calories: 405	Carbs: 29 grams	Fiber: 5 grams
Fat: 19 grams	Protein: 34 grams	Sugar: 6 grams

lamb and apricot tagine

FOR 2 OR 3 SERVINGS

Tagine is a Moroccan couscous dish that mixes sweet, savory, and spicy. The ras el hanout spice blend is a mix of turmeric, cinnamon, cumin, and ginger, and the dried fruit in this dish adds a sweetness that complements the spices. Enjoy!

1 pound sustainably raised lamb shoulder, leg, or stew meat, trimmed and cut into 1-inch cubes

Kosher salt and freshly ground black pepper

2 tablespoons avocado oil

1 medium yellow onion, cut into ¼-inch dice

3 garlic cloves, thinly sliced

2 tablespoons ras el hanout spice blend

2 tablespoons tomato paste

1 cup low-sodium chicken stock

1 (14-ounce) can diced tomatoes

½ cup dried apricots

¼ cup raisins

1 unwaxed lemon, for zesting

⅓ cup chopped fresh cilantro, plus more for garnish

3 cups cooked couscous or quinoa, for serving

⅓ cup sliced almonds, for garnish

1. Preheat the oven to 300°F.

2. Season the lamb on all sides with 1 teaspoon each of salt and pepper.

3. Heat a large Dutch oven over medium-high. Add 1 tablespoon of the oil to the pan. When the oil is shimmering, add half the lamb in an even layer. Brown on all sides, 8 to 10 minutes. Remove from the pan and repeat with the remaining meat.

4. Add the remaining 1 tablespoon oil to the empty pan and heat until shimmering. Add the onion and cook, stirring occasionally, until soft and caramelized, about 3 minutes. Season with salt and pepper. Little bits of the onion will stick to the bottom of the pan; make sure to scrape these up with a wooden spoon to incorporate them. Add the garlic, stir, and cook until fragrant, about 2 minutes. Add the ras el hanout and stir-fry until the spices are fragrant, about 1 minute.

5. Add the tomato paste and stir to coat the vegetables. Cook until the paste is dark, about 2 minutes. Add the chicken stock and deglaze the pan.

6. Add the diced tomatoes, apricots, and raisins and stir to combine. Place the meat back in the pot, season with more salt and pepper, and stir. Bring to a boil and cover with a lid.

7. Place the Dutch oven in the oven and bake until the sauce reduces to a thick paste and the meat pulls apart easily with a fork, 2 to 3 hours.

8. Before serving, zest the lemon over the tagine and add the cilantro. Taste for seasoning and add more salt and pepper, if needed.

9. Serve over couscous, topped with sliced almonds and extra cilantro.

NUTRITION, per serving

| Calories: 694 | Carbs: 96 grams | Fiber: 10 grams |
| Fat: 18 grams | Protein: 39 grams | Sugar: 24 grams |

bites

"

Try to stay open to new experiences, opportunities, relationships ... and, of course, snacks.

"

take a bite

These are great snacks to have on hand; they can stand up to your hangriest moments. You'll always be ready to face whatever comes your way with these quick and easy bites, perfect to take on the go.

3 energy bites for fall

EACH RECIPE MAKES 15 BITES

Energy bites are the perfect satisfying snack with protein, carbs, and healthy fats. Eat them as a midafternoon pick-me-up, before a workout, or as a sweet treat after dinner. Keep them in the fridge for up to 5 days to enjoy throughout the week.

steps for making energy bites

1. In a medium bowl, combine all the ingredients and mix until evenly distributed.

2. Chill in the refrigerator for 30 minutes.

3. Use a tablespoon to scoop out heaping spoonfuls of the mixture, then roll into balls with your hands, making about 15 total. Store in an airtight container in the refrigerator for up to 5 days.

pecan cranberry bites

Vitamin C and potassium in the cranberries make these bites stand out. Plus, the pecans add a nutty flavor and crunchy texture.

⅓ cup dried cranberries

⅔ cup almond butter

¼ cup maple syrup

1 teaspoon pure vanilla extract

1 cup rolled oats

2 tablespoons chopped pecans

Pinch of sea salt

apple pie bites

Easier to make and more nutritious than actual apple pie, these bites will satisfy your sweet craving while giving you a major dose of healthy fats thanks to the almond butter. The cinnamon can reduce inflammation, has antioxidant effects, and fights harmful bacteria.

⅓ cup grated green apple, excess liquid squeezed out

⅓ cup almond butter

¼ cup maple syrup or raw honey

1 teaspoon pure vanilla extract

1½ cups rolled oats

1 teaspoon cinnamon

Pinch of sea salt

pumpkin pie bites

These tasty bites will make you feel like it's sweater weather all year long. Pumpkin is high in nutrients, including beta-carotene, which boosts your immune system, protects your eyesight, and gives you healthy, glowing skin.

⅓ cup pumpkin purée

⅓ cup almond butter

¼ cup maple syrup or raw honey

1 teaspoon pure vanilla extract

1½ cups rolled oats

¼ teaspoon cinnamon

¼ teaspoon grated nutmeg

¼ teaspoon ground ginger

Pinch of sea salt

NUTRITION, per 1 Pecan Cranberry Bite

| Calories: 121 | Carbs: 12 grams | Fiber: 2 grams |
| Fat: 7 grams | Protein: 3 grams | Sugar: 6 grams |

NUTRITION, per 1 Apple Pie Bite

| Calories: 61 | Carbs: 7 grams | Fiber: 1 gram |
| Fat: 3 grams | Protein: 2 grams | Sugar: 4 grams |

NUTRITION, per 1 Pumpkin Pie Bite

| Calories: 61 | Carbs: 7 grams | Fiber: 1 gram |
| Fat: 3 grams | Protein: 2 grams | Sugar: 4 grams |

fruit and seed rollers

VG

If you remember eating fruit leathers or Fruit Roll-Ups as a kid, then these rollers will have you feeling nostalgic. This grown-up version is made with pure fruit but still boasts that great gummy texture that takes you right back to simpler days.

steps for making fruit and seed rollers

1. Preheat the oven to 175°F. Line an 18 × 13-inch baking sheet with a reusable baking mat.

2. Place the fruit, seeds, and honey in a food processor or blender and purée into a thick, smooth sauce.

3. Pour the sauce onto the prepared baking sheet and smooth it into a very thin, even layer that goes almost to the edges of the mat.

4. Bake until the entire surface is just dry to the touch, 4 to 6 hours, for Strawberry Chia and Mango Hemp rollers; bake 5 hours for Blueberry Flax rollers. After 4 hours, start checking every 30 minutes, as the timing depends on the juiciness of the fruit and on how thinly you spread the purée.

5. Remove from the oven and cool completely. Once cool, turn the baking mat onto a cutting board and remove the mat from the fruit sheet.

6. Roll up the fruit sheet and cut it into 1-inch strips.

NOTE

If your fruit sheet comes out a bit too dry and you worry that rolling it up will cause it to crack, simply cover the surface with a few damp paper towels for a few minutes and try again.

strawberry chia

MAKES ABOUT 2 CUPS OF PURÉE

Chia seeds are loaded with fiber, protein, and omega-3 fatty acids. They pair perfectly with the sweetness of the strawberries.

3 cups strawberries, hulled

1 tablespoon chia seeds

2 tablespoons raw honey

mango hemp

MAKES ABOUT 2½ CUPS OF PURÉE

This fruit and seed roller contains vitamin C–rich mango and hemp seeds, which are a full suite of minerals, and protein.

3 cups diced mango, about 1 pound

1 tablespoon hemp seeds

1 tablespoon raw honey

blueberry flax

MAKES ABOUT 2 CUPS OF PURÉE

Blueberries are known as a superfood because of their high antioxidant content. We love mixing these gorgeous deep blue berries with flaxseed for extra protein and fiber.

3 cups blueberries, about 1 pound

1 tablespoon ground flaxseed

1 tablespoon raw honey

NUTRITION, per 1 Strawberry Chia Roll

Calories: 29	Carbs: 7 grams	Fiber: 1 gram
Fat: 1 gram	Protein: 1 gram	Sugar: 5 grams

NUTRITION, per 1 Mango Hemp Roll

Calories: 35	Carbs: 8 grams	Fiber: 1 gram
Fat: 1 gram	Protein: 1 grams	Sugar: 7 grams

NUTRITION, per 1 Blueberry Flax Roll

Calories: 31	Carbs: 7 grams	Fiber: 1 gram
Fat: 1 gram	Protein: 1 gram	Sugar: 5 grams

quinoa super seed crackers

V GF

MAKES 24 CRACKERS

Boxed crackers are often made with processed ingredients, so next time you're craving something crunchy, try making your own! These are full of seeds that are high in healthy fats, fiber, and protein. Serve them with dips or spreads and alongside meats and cheeses.

⅓ cup chia seeds

¾ cup water

¾ cup cooked quinoa

⅓ cup raw pepitas (pumpkin seeds)

⅓ cup sesame seeds

½ teaspoon kosher salt

¼ teaspoon freshly ground black pepper

Hummus or charcuterie and cheese, for serving

1. Preheat the oven to 325°F. Line a baking sheet with a reusable baking mat or parchment paper.

2. In a medium bowl, place the chia seeds and water. Mix until well combined and let stand until the seeds have a gelatinous texture, about 5 minutes.

3. In a large bowl, combine the quinoa, pepitas, sesame seeds, salt, pepper, and chia seed mixture.

4. Transfer onto the prepared baking sheet with a spatula. Spread into a 13 × 10-inch rectangle, a little more than ⅛ inch thick.

5. Bake until the mixture is dried out on top and holds together as one piece, about 30 minutes. Remove from the oven (keep the oven on) and cut into 24 pieces. (Cutting the crackers with a bench scraper lets you do it directly on the baking sheet.) Carefully flip each cracker and spread them out on the baking sheet.

6. Bake until the crackers are crispy throughout, about 30 minutes more. Remove and allow to cool for 10 minutes.

7. These go great with hummus or a charcuterie and cheese plate. Store in an airtight container for up to 1 month.

NUTRITION, per 2-cracker serving

| Calories: 67 | Carbs: 7 grams | Fiber: 3 grams |
| Fat: 4 grams | Protein: 2 grams | Sugar: 0 grams |

southwestern quinoa grain bowl

FOR 6 SERVINGS

This is a great make-ahead salad that packs up well for a hike or an afternoon pick-me-up at your desk. Quinoa is a seed that is prepared and eaten like a grain. Beans add fiber and protein to this bowl, and the corn gives it a hint of sweetness.

2 tablespoons vegetable oil

3 garlic cloves, minced

1 medium jalapeño, seeded and minced

1 (15-ounce) can no-salt-added black beans, drained and rinsed

1 (15-ounce) can corn, drained

3 Roma tomatoes, diced

1 cup uncooked quinoa, rinsed

2 cups low-sodium vegetable stock

1 tablespoon chili powder

2 teaspoons cumin

1 teaspoon kosher salt

1 teaspoon freshly ground black pepper

1 large avocado, cubed

Juice of 1 large lime (about 2 tablespoons)

Freshly chopped cilantro

1. In a large pan, heat the oil over medium. Add the garlic and jalapeño and cook, stirring constantly, until softened, about 2 minutes.

2. Add the black beans, corn, tomatoes, quinoa, stock, chili powder, cumin, salt, and pepper and stir to combine. Bring to a simmer and cook for 15 to 20 minutes, until the liquid is absorbed and the quinoa is tender, adjusting the heat as needed to maintain a simmer. Remove the pan from the heat, give the quinoa a stir, then cover and allow to sit for about 5 minutes.

3. Transfer to a serving bowl and top with the avocado, lime juice, and cilantro. Pack any leftovers in an airtight glass container or jar and refrigerate for up to 5 days.

NUTRITION, per serving

| Calories: 350 | Carbs: 53 grams | Fiber: 13 grams |
| Fat: 12 grams | Protein: 14 grams | Sugar: 6 grams |

low-carb everything pizza bites

GF DF

MAKES 20 BITES

Pizza doesn't have to mean not nutritious! These pizza bites still deliver the full pizza experience without the crust. Pepperoni or salami take the place of the crust, and a muffin tin molds it into place. Add your favorite pizza toppings, and voilà!

1½ teaspoons avocado oil or cooking oil of choice

½ medium yellow onion, finely diced

½ red bell pepper, seeded and finely diced

¼ cup finely diced stemmed cremini or shiitake mushrooms (about 3 mushrooms)

Kosher salt and freshly ground black pepper

1 cup low-sugar marinara sauce

20 slices uncured "sandwich-style" pepperoni or salami, 3 inches in diameter

½ cup shredded dairy-free cheese

Small basil leaves, for garnish

1. Preheat the oven to 400°F.

2. In a small saucepan over medium heat, add the oil and heat for about 1 minute. Add the onion, bell pepper, and mushrooms and season with salt and black pepper. Cook until the vegetables soften, about 5 minutes. Add the marinara sauce and simmer for about 10 minutes more.

3. Using two 12-cup mini-muffin tins, or making the pepperoni bites in one tin in two batches, press 1 pepperoni slice into each muffin cup, making sure to press the pepperoni slice into the bottom and up the sides to form a cup. It's okay if the pepperoni slice overlaps itself a little bit. Spoon 1 tablespoon of the vegetable marinara into each pepperoni cup. Sprinkle with 1 heaping teaspoon of cheese per cup.

4. Bake until the cheese is melted and the edges of the pepperoni are crisp, 10 to 12 minutes. Remove from the oven and let cool for 10 minutes before transferring the pepperoni cups to a plate.

5. Sprinkle the basil over the pizza cups.

NUTRITION, per 4-piece serving

| Calories: 268 | Carbs: 7 grams | Fiber: 1 gram |
| Fat: 22 grams | Protein: 10 grams | Sugar: 4 grams |

fall slaw

V

A sophisticated version of traditional coleslaw thanks to the sweet-and-sour tahini–poppy seed dressing, this super-colorful slaw is perfect for a picnic or potluck. The Brussels sprouts and all of the other veggies in this dish make it a nutritional powerhouse. Go ahead and take this slaw to your family barbecue or to a get-together with friends.

SLAW

12 large Brussels sprouts

2 large carrots

1 medium red beet, peeled

6 large radishes

½ large red onion

½ medium head cauliflower, cut into small florets (about 2 heaping cups)

1 large Fuji apple, thinly sliced (about 2 cups)

1 teaspoon kosher salt

½ cup raw pistachios, roughly chopped

TAHINI–POPPY SEED DRESSING (MAKES ABOUT 1½ CUPS)

6 tablespoons cider vinegar

⅓ cup tahini, well stirred

¼ cup maple syrup

½ teaspoon cayenne pepper

3 medium garlic cloves

Kosher salt

⅓ cup extra-virgin olive oil

Cold water, as needed

2 tablespoons poppy seeds

1. Into a large bowl, grate the Brussels sprouts, carrots, and beets using the grating insert of a mandoline or the large holes of a box grater.

2. Thinly slice the radishes and onion with the slicing insert of the mandoline or a sharp knife and add to the bowl with the other vegetables.

3. Add the cauliflower and apple to the bowl, season with salt, and toss to combine.

4. In a small sauté pan over medium heat, toast the pistachios, stirring frequently, until they are lightly browned and smell nutty, 3 to 5 minutes. Set aside.

5. In a blender, combine the vinegar, tahini, maple syrup, cayenne, garlic, and a large pinch of salt. Blend until smooth. With the blender running, drizzle in the oil to emulsify. Add cold water as needed to thin the dressing to your desired consistency. Add the poppy seeds and pulse to incorporate. Taste and season with more salt if needed.

6. If eating in the next few hours, toss the slaw with the dressing and the toasted pistachios. The slaw will keep at room temperature for up to 2 hours, or in the refrigerator for 1 day with the dressing or 3 days without.

NUTRITION, per 1-cup serving

| Calories: 215 | Carbs: 18 grams | Fiber: 4 grams |
| Fat: 15 grams | Protein: 5 grams | Sugar: 10 grams |

15-minute black bean, corn, and queso fresco quesadilla

VG

FOR 2 SERVINGS

This is one of those great pantry meals—a recipe you can make using mostly ingredients you might already have. It's a good idea to keep canned beans on hand for recipes like this—buy the versions in BPA-free cans, and even better if they're organic. Quesadillas are quick, easy, and can be customized with whatever you have in the refrigerator or pantry.

1 (15-ounce) can no-salt-added black beans, drained and rinsed

¼ cup frozen corn

¼ cup jarred salsa

3 or 4 dashes of hot sauce (optional)

Kosher salt

2 (8½-inch) flaxseed tortillas

Nonstick cooking spray

½ cup packed crumbled queso fresco cheese

½ avocado, sliced, for serving

1. Place a medium to large skillet over medium heat. When the skillet is hot, add ⅓ cup of the black beans, the corn, salsa, and hot sauce, if using. Season with salt. Stir and cook until the beans and corn are cooked through and the salsa and hot sauce have reduced, 2 to 3 minutes. When there is no excess liquid left, transfer the filling to a bowl.

2. Wipe out the skillet and place it back over medium heat. Spray each tortilla on one side with nonstick cooking spray.

3. Lay a tortilla spray-side down in the skillet and sprinkle with half of the cheese. Spoon on the filling and top with the remaining cheese. Lay a second tortilla on top, spray-side up. Cook until the bottom tortilla is golden brown, 2 to 3 minutes, then flip and cook the other side of the quesadilla for 2 to 3 minutes. If any filling falls out when flipping, just lift the side and push the filling back in. The quesadilla is done when the cheese is melted and the second tortilla is golden brown.

4. Remove the quesadilla from the skillet and allow it to cool for 1 minute before cutting into 8 wedges. Serve with the avocado slices.

NUTRITION, per serving

| Calories: 557 | Carbs: 80 grams | Fiber: 27 grams |
| Total fat: 16 grams | Protein: 28 grams | Sugar: 2 grams |

puffed quinoa cacao bites

V GF

MAKES 20 BITES

Cacao beans are the seeds of the cacao tree and are the purest form of chocolate. Cacao is high in antioxidants, vitamins, minerals, and amino acids. More important, it has emotional benefits: its polyphenols reduce anxiety, so you should reach for these bites to create a moment of calm. This recipe includes an easy trick for making your own puffed quinoa, but you can also make this with your preferred store-bought variety.

1 cup uncooked quinoa

2 teaspoons coconut oil

⅓ cup almond butter

¾ cup pitted Medjool dates, minced (about 10 dates)

¼ cup cacao nibs

½ teaspoon cinnamon

Pinch of kosher salt

1. In a medium bowl, cover the quinoa by 2 inches with cool water. Soak in the refrigerator for at least 6 hours and up to overnight.

2. The next morning, put a baking sheet in the oven and preheat the oven to 250°F.

3. Over a medium bowl, strain the quinoa through a fine-mesh sieve, shaking off as much excess liquid as possible. Pour the damp quinoa onto the preheated baking sheet and spread it into an even layer.

4. Bake until the quinoa is completely dry, 10 to 15 minutes, stirring once halfway through. Remove from the oven and set aside to cool completely, 15 to 20 minutes.

5. In a large Dutch oven over medium-high heat, melt 1 teaspoon of the coconut oil. Add half the quinoa and toast, stirring frequently, until most of the seeds have popped and are lightly golden brown, 5 to 8 minutes. When done, they will have the color of toasted sesame seeds. The quinoa will pop, similar to popcorn in sound but not movement; the pop is not nearly as wild. Pour the popped quinoa into a large bowl and allow to cool completely. Repeat with the remaining 1 teaspoon oil and the other half of the quinoa.

6. Add the almond butter, dates, cacao nibs, cinnamon, and salt to the quinoa. Stir to combine. Pinch off bite-size pieces (about 1 heaping tablespoon) and squeeze the mixture in the palm of your hand until it holds together. Press and roll the mixture into balls, making about 20 total. Place in the refrigerator until solid, at least 2 hours or up to overnight.

7. Store in an airtight container in the refrigerator for up to 1 week or in the freezer for up to 3 months.

NUTRITION, per 5-bite serving

| Calories: 439 | Carbs: 55 grams | Fiber: 10 grams |
| Fat: 21 grams | Protein: 12 grams | Sugar: 20 grams |

pumpkin seed cashew bites

V

MAKES 36 BITES

These bites are made with barley malt, which is a natural sweetener made from soaked and sprouted barley, and can be used in place of molasses, honey, or maple syrup. It offers more nutrients than granulated white sugar, although you should be aware that it contains gluten. The organic versions tend to be processed in an old-fashioned way that leaves most nutrients intact, so keep your eye out for the "organic" label. Here it's combined with crunchy seeds and nuts for a quick, nourishing bite.

2 cups raw unsalted cashews, 1 cup roughly chopped and the rest left whole

1 cup raw pepitas (pumpkin seeds)

1 cup raw unsalted almonds, roughly chopped

1½ teaspoons kosher salt

½ cup organic barley malt syrup

1 cup puffed rice cereal

Nonstick cooking spray

1. Preheat the oven to 350°F. Line a 9 × 9-inch pan with parchment paper.

2. In a medium bowl, combine the cashews, pepitas, almonds, salt, barley syrup, and cereal. Thoroughly stir to ensure the syrup evenly coats everything.

3. Pour into the prepared pan. Lightly spray the outer bottom of a measuring cup with nonstick cooking spray. Using the measuring cup, press the mixture tightly into the pan and flatten the top.

4. Bake until aromatic and golden brown, and the edges appear set, 15 to 20 minutes. Remove from the oven and let cool for at least 30 minutes.

5. When cool, run a paring knife around the edges of the pan. Place a cutting board on top of the pan and flip the pan over to release the nut mixture, then remove the parchment paper. Cut into 36 pieces: First cut six columns about 1½ inches wide, then cut each column into six squares, every ½ inch. Store in an airtight container, with parchment between each layer, for up to 10 days.

NUTRITION, per 2 bite serving

| Calories: 184 | Carbs: 16 grams | Fiber: 2 grams |
| Fat: 12 grams | Protein: 5 grams | Sugar: 8 grams |

dark chocolate coconut almond energy bites

V GF

MAKES 24 BITES

This is an indulgent bite full of antioxidants and healthy fats for sustained energy. Almonds, coconut, and dark chocolate are a classic combination—think of this as an unprocessed and deconstructed candy bar treat.

Nonstick cooking spray

1 cup roughly chopped unsalted almonds

1 cup unsweetened coconut flakes

2 tablespoons chia seeds

1 teaspoon kosher salt

½ cup maple syrup

1 cup vegan dark chocolate chunks or chips

1 tablespoon coconut oil

1. Preheat the oven to 350°F. Line two 12-cup mini-muffin tins with reusable silicone liners or use two mini-muffin silicone molds. Grease the molds with nonstick cooking spray.

2. In a medium bowl, combine the almonds, coconut flakes, chia seeds, and salt. Pour in the maple syrup. Stir to combine.

3. Spoon a heaping tablespoon into each muffin cup. Pack down very tightly. Evenly distribute any remaining mixture and press down firmly to pack the cups. The mixture should just fill the cups.

4. Bake until the bites are golden brown and bubbling around the edges, 13 to 15 minutes. Remove from the oven and set aside to cool for at least 30 minutes.

5. In a small microwave-safe bowl, add the chocolate chunks and coconut oil. Microwave for 30 seconds. Stir, then microwave for another 30 seconds. Stir again until smooth; if the chocolate is not yet melted, microwave again in 10-second intervals until smooth. You can also place the chocolate and oil in a heatproof bowl and place it over a pot with boiling water. Stir the chocolate and oil until melted and evenly combined, 60 to 90 seconds.

6. Spoon the melted chocolate over each bite, about 1½ teaspoons per bite, covering the top entirely in an even layer. If there is any extra chocolate, evenly spread it over the bites, filling any holes. Refrigerate until the chocolate is set, about 1 hour, or freeze for about 15 minutes.

7. Store in an airtight container in the refrigerator for up to 2 weeks or in the freezer for up to 6 months.

NUTRITION, per 2-bite serving

| Calories: 245 | Carbs: 22 grams | Fiber: 4 grams |
| Fat: 17 grams | Protein: 4 grams | Sugar: 16 grams |

better-for-you air-popped popcorn

MAKES 7 CUPS

A classic snack! Popcorn is naturally high-fiber and low-calorie, but store-bought versions contain non-nutritious ingredients like chemical preservatives and flavorings, trans fats, and excess sodium. This homemade popcorn tastes great with only pure, wholesome ingredients, and you can choose your own adventure with the toppings. We see a movie night in your future!

¼ cup popcorn kernels

1 brown paper lunch bag

Kosher salt

1. Pour the kernels into the paper bag.

2. Tightly fold the top of the bag over by an inch, then fold the bag down again by another inch. Fold the two corners tightly down toward the center of the bag. This will ensure the kernels don't spill out.

3. Place the bag, fold-side down, in the microwave and heat on high for about 1 minute 30 seconds. Listen to the popping; when there are 2 seconds between each pop, stop the microwave.

4. Remove the bag from the microwave and open the bag, being careful of the steam coming out. Season with salt for plain popcorn or add the popcorn to a large bowl, toss with butter, oil, or honey; your seasoning of choice; and/or salt to taste. Serve immediately.

SUGGESTED TOPPINGS

2 tablespoons grated Parmesan cheese and 2 tablespoons unsalted grass-fed butter, melted

1 tablespoon Everything Seasoning (page 37) and 2 tablespoons coconut oil, melted

2 tablespoons furikake seasoning and 1 to 2 tablespoons chili oil or toasted sesame oil, depending on your desired spice level

1 teaspoon cinnamon and 2 tablespoons raw honey

1½ teaspoons finely minced rosemary leaves and 2 tablespoons extra-virgin olive oil

NUTRITION, per 1-cup serving (plain)

| Calories: 44 | Carbs: 4 grams | Fiber: 1 grams |
| Fat: 3 gram | Protein: 1 grams | Sugar: 0 grams |

NUTRITION, per 1-cup serving (butter Parmesan)

| Calories: 80 | Carbs: 5 grams | Fiber: 1 gram |
| Fat: 6 grams | Protein: 1 gram | Sugar: 0 grams |

NUTRITION, per 1-cup serving (Everything Seasoning)

| Calories: 79 | Carbs: 4 grams | Fiber: 1 gram |
| Fat: 7 grams | Protein: 1 grams | Sugar: 0 grams |

NUTRITION, per 1-cup serving (furikake sesame)

| Calories: 82 | Carbs: 5 grams | Fiber: 1 gram |
| Fat: 7 grams | Protein: 1 gram | Sugar: 0 grams |

NUTRITION, per 1-cup serving (cinnamon honey)

| Calories: 62 | Carbs: 10 grams | Fiber: 1 gram |
| Fat: 3 grams | Protein: 1 gram | Sugar: 5 grams |

NUTRITION, per 1-cup serving (rosemary olive oil)

| Calories: 78 | Carbs: 4 grams | Fiber: 1 gram |
| Fat: 7 grams | Protein: 1 gram | Sugar: 0 grams |

5-minute mint, pea, and feta salad (VG) (GF)

FOR 1 SERVING

This is a super flexible little salad to have in your back pocket for a quick dose of yummy veggies. You can easily double or triple its size for a crowd or for meal prep. It's delicious warm or cold. We recommend adding sliced almonds, pine nuts, or walnuts for extra crunch. However you enjoy it, the peas are a great source of plant-based protein and filling fiber.

1 cup frozen peas

1 teaspoon extra-virgin olive oil

Pinch of kosher salt

Pinch of crushed red pepper flakes (optional)

Juice of ½ lemon (2 tablespoons)

6 mint leaves, sliced

1 tablespoon crumbled feta cheese

Handful of snap peas, for garnish (optional)

1. In a medium microwave-safe bowl, place the peas, oil, salt, and red pepper flakes, if using. Microwave on high for 90 seconds. Stir to distribute the heat, then heat again until the peas are warmed through, about 1 minute more.

2. Transfer the peas to a serving bowl. Add the lemon juice, mint, and feta, and stir to combine. Garnish with the snap peas, if desired.

NUTRITION

Calories: 225	Carbs: 31 grams	Fiber: 12 grams
Fat: 8 grams	Protein: 12 grams	Sugar: 6 grams

treats

"

Catch those
tiny moments of
contentment and
pleasure that often
slip through
the cracks.

"

how sweet

We know that everyone needs a sweet treat now and then, but that doesn't mean you have to abandon your goals. We've got you! This chapter is full of gluten-free and vegan recipes, as well as not-too-sweet classics. We have simple, wholesome treats for indulgences, celebrations, and when a craving hits.

chai-spiced polenta cake

VG **GF**

This luscious cake is made with fragrant and robust chai tea, finely ground polenta, and sweet-tart plums. Polenta is ground cornmeal and chai spice is a wonderful blend of cardamom, cinnamon, nutmeg, and cloves. Completely free of refined sugars, this cake gets its sweetness from the cornmeal, maple syrup, and plums. Delicious!

1 cup extra-virgin olive oil, plus more for greasing

1½ cups finely ground yellow cornmeal

1½ cups superfine almond flour

1 teaspoon baking powder

½ teaspoon baking soda

Pinch of kosher salt

Zest and juice of 1 large orange (about 1½ teaspoons zest and ¼ cup juice), plus extra zest for optional garnish

4 large free-range eggs, beaten

½ cup plus 2 tablespoons maple syrup

1 teaspoon pure vanilla extract

1 teaspoon ground cardamom

1 teaspoon cinnamon

½ teaspoon grated nutmeg

½ teaspoon ground cloves

3 plums: 2 pitted and diced, 1 sliced into ½-inch wedges

Whipped cream, for serving

1. Preheat the oven to 350°F. Grease a 9-inch round nonstick cake pan with oil, using a paper towel to spread it evenly. If you don't have a nonstick pan, you can grease the bottom of a regular cake pan, line it with parchment paper, and then grease the top of the parchment as well.

2. In a large bowl, combine the cornmeal, flour, baking powder, baking soda, and salt. Stir well.

3. In a separate large bowl, add the orange zest and juice, eggs, olive oil, maple syrup, vanilla, cardamom, cinnamon, nutmeg, and cloves. Whisk well to combine.

4. Add the dry ingredients to the wet ingredients and gently fold with a rubber spatula until fully incorporated.

5. Fold in the diced plums. Pour the batter into the prepared pan. Arrange the sliced plum decoratively on top of the cake in a circular pattern.

6. Bake the cake until a toothpick inserted into the center comes out clean, 50 minutes to 1 hour.

7. Let cool for 20 minutes, then remove from the cake pan.

8. Cut into 8 slices and serve with whipped cream and more orange zest, if desired.

NUTRITION, per slice

| Calories: 542 | Carbs: 28 grams | Fiber: 4 grams |
| Fat: 45 grams | Protein: 10 grams | Sugar: 17 grams |

4-ingredient truffles

MAKES 35 TO 40 TRUFFLES

These simple truffles can be topped with almost anything your heart desires! The base uses four nutritious ingredients. The dark chocolate is rich in antioxidants, is a natural mood booster, and loses all its bitterness with the preparation, so no sugar or dairy is required. The coconut binds it together, with vanilla extract and salt for the perfect bite.

TRUFFLES

1 cup full-fat unsweetened coconut milk, mixed well before measuring

20 ounces dark chocolate, chopped

1 teaspoon pure vanilla extract

Pinch of kosher salt

SUGGESTED TOPPINGS

Cocoa powder

Crushed pistachios

Unsweetened coconut flakes

Crushed hazelnuts

Freeze-dried strawberries

Matcha powder

1. In a small saucepan over medium heat, bring the coconut milk to a simmer. In a medium heatproof bowl, place the chopped chocolate. Pour the warm coconut milk over the chopped chocolate and stir until melted and smooth.

2. Add the vanilla and salt and use a rubber spatula to combine. If the chocolate does not melt completely, microwave on high in 10-second intervals until the mixture is smooth when stirred together.

3. Cover and cool in the refrigerator until set, about 2 hours. When you press the mixture with your fingertip, it should leave an indentation. Do not chill for too long—the mixture will be extremely difficult to scoop if it hardens too much.

4. Using a 1-tablespoon measuring spoon, portion out the truffle mixture and place on a baking sheet.

5. Roll each truffle between your palms to create a sphere. The outside should be slightly tacky from the heat of your palms. This will help the toppings to stick. (Your hands will get messy during this process.) If the truffles get too soft, place in the refrigerator for about 10 minutes. Roll the truffles in the toppings of your choice.

6. Serve immediately, or refrigerate for about 1 hour for firmer truffles. Uncoated truffle balls will keep in an airtight container in the fridge for up to 10 days; coat them in the toppings just before serving.

NUTRITION, per 2 truffles (no toppings)

| Calories: 205 | Carbs: 20 grams | Fiber: 1 gram |
| Fat: 12 grams | Protein: 2 grams | Sugar: 16 grams |

fudgy hidden-veggie brownies

FOR 9 SERVINGS

Fudge brownies *and* vegetables? Yup, we went there! This version of brownies sneaks in a dose of veggies—and it's grain- and refined sugar–free to boot. The sweet potatoes don't just add potassium and fiber—they also make these brownies moist and delicious. Go ahead and try it!

Nonstick cooking spray

2 small or 1 large sweet potato, 1 pound total

1⅓ cups semisweet chocolate chips

⅓ cup chopped unsweetened chocolate

6 tablespoons maple syrup

1 teaspoon pure vanilla extract

3 large free-range eggs

1 cup superfine almond flour

¼ cup unsweetened Dutch-processed cocoa powder

½ teaspoon kosher salt

1. Preheat the oven to 350°F. Lightly grease an 8 × 8-inch baking dish with nonstick cooking spray.

2. Cut the sweet potatoes in half lengthwise and place them cut-side up in a microwave-safe dish. Cook on high for 7 minutes, then leave in the microwave for 5 minutes. If the middle is still hard, cook for about 2 minutes more.

3. Carefully scoop the sweet potato flesh into a food processor. Compost or discard the skin. You will have about 1½ cups sweet potato flesh.

4. To the food processor, add ¾ cup of the chocolate chips, the unsweetened chocolate, maple syrup, and vanilla. The heat from the sweet potatoes will melt the chocolate.

5. Process until very smooth, scraping down the sides of the bowl as needed, 2 to 3 minutes. The mixture should look like chocolate mousse.

6. In a medium bowl, whisk the eggs, then add the flour, cocoa powder, and salt and whisk to combine. Add the sweet potato mixture and fold with a rubber spatula to combine. Fold in ¼ cup of the chocolate chips. Transfer the batter to the prepared baking dish and smooth the top. Top with the remaining ⅓ cup chocolate chips.

7. Bake until a toothpick inserted into the center of the brownies comes out clean (a few moist crumbs is fine, but there should be no wet batter on the toothpick), 30 to 35 minutes.

8. Let cool completely before slicing. Cut three even rows in one direction, then three in the opposite direction, giving you 9 brownies.

NUTRITION, per brownie

| Calories: 341 | Carbs: 40 grams | Fiber: 6 grams |
| Fat: 19 grams | Protein: 8 grams | Sugar: 25 grams |

baked pear crumble

FOR 8 SERVINGS

Cooking with the seasons connects you to the natural cycles of the earth and keeps your environmental footprint to a minimum. Flexible and forgiving, fruit crumbles can be made throughout the year using whatever is in season. (Check out our seasonal produce chart on page 22.) Different types of pears are at their peak at different times throughout the year. Use Bartlett pears in the summer, Bosc in the fall, and D'Anjou in the winter for this recipe. Whatever the variety, pears combine beautifully with the nutty, crunchy, sweet crumble on top.

1 cup quick-cooking oats

½ cup skin-on hazelnuts

½ cup walnuts

½ cup unsweetened shredded coconut

⅓ cup dried cherries

2 tablespoons flaxseeds

½ teaspoon cinnamon

½ teaspoon kosher salt

¼ cup unrefined coconut oil, melted

3 tablespoons raw honey, plus more for drizzling

½ teaspoon pure vanilla extract

4 ripe pears, such as Bosc, D'Anjou, or Bartlett, about 2½ pounds

Whipped topping of choice, for serving

1. Preheat the oven to 350°F.

2. In a food processor, combine the oats, hazelnuts, walnuts, coconut, cherries, flaxseeds, cinnamon, and salt. Pulse until finely ground.

3. Add the oil, honey, and vanilla and pulse until just combined. The mixture should hold together when squeezed between your fingers.

4. Cut the pears in half lengthwise. Using a tablespoon, scoop out the cores. With a paring knife, cut a "V" shape around the edges of the stem, cutting downward on an angle. Remove the stems.

5. Set the pears in a 13 × 9-inch baking dish, cut-side up. Fill each pear with ¼ cup of the crumble topping, pressing it lightly into the pears. Pour in enough water to come ¼ inch up the side of the baking dish.

6. Bake until the topping is golden brown and the pears are tender when pierced with a paring knife, 35 to 45 minutes.

7. Serve immediately, topped with whipped topping and a drizzle of honey.

NUTRITION, per serving

| Calories: 305 | Carbs: 30 grams | Fiber: 6 grams |
| Fat: 21 grams | Protein: 4 grams | Sugar: 19 grams |

hazelnut-crusted brie-and-pear tart

FOR 12 SERVINGS

This fresh and savory dessert is the way to class up your next potluck or book club meeting. Brie cheese, rosemary, and orange marmalade are heavenly together. The hazelnut crust is crunchy and light. Your crew will love this paired with a glass of sparkling water or a bottle of fruity dry rosé.

Leaves from 1 large sprig rosemary (about 1 tablespoon)

1 cup toasted hazelnuts, about 5 ounces, toasted, skins removed

1 cup buckwheat flour

4 tablespoons maple syrup

⅛ teaspoon kosher salt

4 tablespoons (½ stick) unsalted grass-fed butter, cubed and chilled

3 tablespoons orange marmalade

4 ounces Brie cheese, thinly sliced (10 to 12 pieces)

6 cups thinly sliced pears (3 to 4 pears)

1. Preheat the oven to 400°F.

2. In a food processor, combine the rosemary, hazelnuts, flour, 3 tablespoons of the maple syrup, and the salt. Pulse until the hazelnuts break down and the mixture resembles a coarse meal.

3. Add the butter and pulse until no large chunks of butter remain.

4. Lightly grease a 10-inch tart pan with a removable bottom. Press the dough into the pan and poke holes all over the dough with a fork.

5. Bake the crust until lightly browned around the edges, 10 to 15 minutes.

6. Reduce the oven temperature to 375°F.

7. Gently spread the orange marmalade over the warm crust. Arrange the Brie slices evenly over the marmalade.

8. Shingle the pear slices neatly around the outside edge of the tart, packing them close together. Add a second layer around the outside edge on top of the first layer. There should be a circle left in the center of the tart. Begin tucking pear slices horizontally, skin-side up, around the edge of the inner circle. Work toward the center, using smaller slices as the circle gets smaller (the thinner, the better here; very thin slices will bend and not break). Once you reach the center, tuck a few small slices into the center to fill it in.

9. Using a pastry brush, lightly coat the pears with the remaining 1 tablespoon maple syrup.

10. Bake until the pears have softened, about 40 minutes.

11. Cool for at least 30 minutes before slicing.

NUTRITION, per serving

| Calories: 226 | Carbs: 25 grams | Fiber: 4 grams |
| Fat: 13 grams | Protein: 5 grams | Sugar: 13 grams |

banana nice cream, 3 ways

Frozen bananas prove magic is real. When bananas get too ripe to eat, freeze them for these gorgeous nice creams! If you don't fancy banana-flavored ice cream night after night, don't worry. Banana is just the base for you to riff on with your favorite flavor combos.

steps for making banana nice cream

1. Peel the bananas, cut them into coins, and place in a reusable zip-top bag. Freeze overnight or until solid.

2. Place all the ingredients in a food processor or blender and blend until smooth.

3. Pour the contents of the blender into a loaf pan or other small pan.

4. Freeze until the texture is similar to a rich, creamy ice cream, at least 1 hour. If frozen overnight, remove from the freezer and allow to soften at room temperature for 20 to 30 minutes before serving.

vanilla bean nice cream

FOR 4 SERVINGS; MAKES ABOUT 2 CUPS

3 ripe bananas, about 1½ pounds unpeeled

¼ cup milk of choice

Seeds from 1 vanilla bean (⅛ teaspoon)

NUTRITION, per serving

Calories: 96	Carbs: 23 grams	Fiber: 3 grams
Fat: 1 gram	Protein: 2 grams	Sugar: 12 grams

chocolate peanut butter nice cream

FOR 4 SERVINGS; MAKES ABOUT 2 CUPS

3 ripe bananas, about 1½ pounds unpeeled

2 tablespoons creamy peanut butter

1 tablespoon unsweetened cocoa powder

¼ cup milk of choice

NUTRITION, per serving

Calories: 148	Carbs: 26 grams	Fiber: 3 grams
Fat: 5 grams	Protein: 4 grams	Sugar: 13 grams

cacao nib mint nice cream

FOR 4 SERVINGS; MAKES ABOUT 2 CUPS

3 bananas, about 1½ pounds unpeeled

½ cup dark cacao nibs

4 mint leaves

Seeds from 1 vanilla bean (⅛ teaspoon)

¼ cup milk of choice

NUTRITION, per serving

Calories: 115	Carbs: 26 grams	Fiber: 3 grams
Fat: 1 gram	Protein: 2 grams	Sugar: 13 grams

coconut strawberry banana pops

These creamy, dreamy pops have major out-of-office vacation vibes, taking you to hot summer days no matter where or when you make them. They're packed with vitamin C and potassium that will make you glow from the inside out. You're welcome!

1 (14-ounce) can full-fat unsweetened coconut milk, well mixed

2 cups diced strawberries

1 banana, sliced (about ¾ cup)

3 tablespoons raw honey

1. Place the coconut milk, strawberries, banana, and honey in a blender and blend until smooth.

2. Divide the mixture among six large ice pop molds (at least 3 ounces each), filling them to the fill line. It might make less or more than six ice pops, depending on the size of the mold you use.

3. Freeze until completely frozen, at least 4 hours and up to overnight.

NUTRITION, per serving

Calories: 198	Carbs: 21 grams	Fiber: 2 grams
Fat: 14 grams	Protein: 2 grams	Sugar: 14 grams

the fudgiest dairy-free chocolate cake

FOR 10 SERVINGS

This cake is vegan as long as you use organic sugar (nonorganic sugar often uses bone char to filter the sugar), and it calls for whole-wheat flour, upping the nutrient density. Really, though, the cake is just pure, rich, chocolatey indulgence. This is great for a big group that includes vegans and dairy queens alike.

FROSTING

2 (15-ounce) cans full-fat unsweetened coconut milk, well mixed

3 cups dairy-free chocolate chips or chunks

¼ cup unrefined coconut oil, melted

2 cups organic confectioners' sugar

CAKE

Nonstick cooking spray

3 cups white whole-wheat flour

1½ cups unsweetened dark cocoa powder

1 cup organic sugar

1 tablespoon baking soda

1½ teaspoons baking powder

Pinch of kosher salt

3 cups unsweetened almond milk

1 cup unrefined coconut oil, melted

1½ cups applesauce

1½ cups maple syrup

1 tablespoon cider vinegar

1 tablespoon pure vanilla extract

Berries, for garnish

1. The night before serving, make the frosting. In a microwave-safe measuring cup or a small pot on the stove, heat the coconut milk until hot but not boiling (about 2 minutes in the microwave on high). Whisk the coconut milk to ensure it's smooth.

2. Place the chocolate in a large bowl and pour the hot coconut milk over it. Let stand for 1 to 2 minutes to allow the milk to melt the chocolate. Mix well.

3. Once the chocolate is melted, add the coconut oil and confectioners' sugar. Beat with a hand mixer or whisk until smooth. Cover and refrigerate overnight.

4. Preheat the oven to 350°F. Grease three 8-inch round cake pans with nonstick cooking spray and set aside.

5. In a large bowl, place the flour, cocoa powder, sugar, baking soda, baking powder, and salt. Whisk to combine and set aside.

6. In a separate large bowl, place the almond milk, coconut oil, applesauce, maple syrup, vinegar, and vanilla. Whisk to combine.

7. In two batches, add the dry ingredients to the wet ingredients, folding with a rubber spatula until combined. Some clumps may form from the coconut oil solidifying again; this is okay since they will melt during baking. Just make sure there are no flour clumps.

RECIPE CONTINUES

8. Divide the batter evenly among the prepared cake pans and bake until a toothpick inserted into the middle comes out almost entirely clean, 35 to 45 minutes. Cool the cakes in the pans until they can be handled and then transfer the cakes to baking sheets lined with a reusable baking mat or parchment paper. Cool the cakes completely.

9. Remove the frosting from the refrigerator and mix well until evenly combined and shiny.

10. Add a tablespoon of frosting to your cake stand. Place small sheets of parchment around the edges of the cake stand to protect the stand from getting messy. Choose which cake will be your bottom layer and place that one in the middle of the stand. Top with 1½ cups of the frosting and evenly spread it to the edges. Top with the second layer, then another 1½ cups of frosting, and spread it evenly to the edges. Add the final layer and frost the top and the sides of the cake generously, garnishing with the berries of your choice. Gently remove the parchment from the edges of the cake stand and serve.

NUTRITION, per serving

| Calories: 725 | Carbs: 94 grams | Fiber: 6 grams |
| Fat: 40 grams | Protein: 7 grams | Sugar: 66 grams |

honey vanilla kefir panna cotta

GF

FOR 8 SERVINGS

Panna cotta is traditionally made with heavy cream, but this recipe uses kefir, which has more protein and more probiotics than Greek yogurt and lends a dreamy creaminess to the dish. This is also made with honey instead of processed sugar, making it a wholesome spin on the Italian classic. This vanilla-flavored dessert makes a fresh, sweet breakfast or a perfect end to a Mediterranean feast.

1½ cups grass-fed whole milk

1 tablespoon grass-fed gelatin, scant 2 (¼-ounce) packages (you won't need all of the second packet)

⅔ cup raw honey

¼ teaspoon kosher salt

1 vanilla bean

2 cups plain unsweetened whole-milk kefir

⅓ cup chopped walnuts, for serving (optional)

Splash of port or sherry, for serving (optional)

1. Into a small bowl, pour ½ cup of the milk and sprinkle in the gelatin. Stir to combine. Set aside for about 5 minutes for the gelatin to bloom.

2. In a medium saucepan, place the remaining 1 cup milk, the honey, and salt.

3. Using a paring knife, split the vanilla bean in half lengthwise. Using the back of the knife scrape out the vanilla seeds and add them to the milk along with the empty pod. Stir.

4. Heat the milk mixture over medium-low. Whisk every few minutes, staying close to the stove so that you can gently heat the milk to just steaming. The milk will curdle if it gets too hot. Once you see the first wisp of steam, remove the pan from the heat.

5. Whisk the bloomed gelatin into the warm milk, stirring until dissolved.

6. Whisk in the kefir.

7. Strain the mixture into a large liquid measuring cup or bowl. (You should have about 4 cups.) Divide evenly among eight 4-ounce ramekins, making sure to leave ¼ inch of space between the mixture and the top of the ramekin. Place the panna cotta in the refrigerator until set, 3 to 4 hours.

8. To unmold, gently dip the ramekins into warm water for about 10 seconds. Place a plate on top, then flip and remove the mold. If it still won't budge, run a paring knife around the edge of the ramekin or dip it in warm water for another 10 seconds. Place the plate on top of the ramekin again and shake left to right, not up and down, until the panna cotta releases. To be honest, you can just eat it out of the mold if you want!

9. Serve with chopped walnuts for breakfast or a splash of port or sherry poured on top for a dinner-party dessert.

NUTRITION, per serving

Calories: 180	Carbs: 30 grams	Fiber: 0 grams
Fat: 5 grams	Protein: 6 grams	Sugar: 29 grams

impossibly good no-churn sorbets

V GF DF

You don't need an ice cream maker for these insanely good sorbets. They take a bit of planning ahead since they need to freeze at least overnight, but the effort will be worth it! You can let your creativity fly with all sorts of flavor combos.

chocolate

FOR 7 SERVINGS

2 cups pure coconut water

1 cup organic sugar

½ cup unsweetened Dutch-processed cocoa powder

½ cup brewed coffee

¼ teaspoon kosher salt

5 ounces dark chocolate, 65 to 80% cocoa content, finely chopped (about ¾ heaping cup)

1. Prep an 8 × 4-inch or 9 × 5-inch loaf pan by lining the entire pan with plastic wrap, pressing firmly against the bottom of the pan and up the sides and making sure there's at least 1 inch of overhang on all sides. You might need to use two sheets of plastic wrap.

2. In a medium saucepan, heat the coconut water, sugar, and cocoa powder over medium. Bring to a boil and whisk to dissolve the sugar and break up any clumps of cocoa powder, about 1 minute. Remove from the heat.

3. Add the coffee and salt, and stir to combine. Add the chocolate to the hot liquid and stir slowly until melted completely.

4. Pour the chocolate mixture over a sieve into the prepared pan in order to catch any lumps. Let the mixture come to room temperature, about 30 minutes. Cover with plastic wrap. Freeze until solid, 6 to 8 hours.

5. Remove from the freezer. Let sit at room temperature for about 1 minute. Gently pull the plastic wrap from the top and then turn the pan over onto a cutting board. Gently pull on a corner of the plastic until the entire sorbet releases. Don't try to force the sorbet out or the plastic will rip; just gently pull and it will release when the sides warm up slightly. Very carefully remove the plastic wrap from the rest of the loaf. With a serrated knife, cut the sorbet into roughly ½- to 1-inch cubes.

6. Place in a food processor and pulse 25 to 30 times, scraping down the sides when necessary. Once all the large chunks are broken down, run the food processor on high until completely smooth. This will do two things: break down large ice crystals and whip air into the mixture. Just don't blend it for so long that the mixture turns to liquid; it should resemble a slushy.

7. Pour the mixture back into an unlined loaf pan, cover with plastic wrap, and freeze until set, another 4 to 5 hours. (This makes 3¼ cups.)

NUTRITION, per ½-cup serving

| Calories: 300 | Carbs: 55 grams | Fiber: 4 grams |
| Fat: 8 grams | Protein: 3 grams | Sugar: 47 grams |

RECIPE CONTINUES

fruit sorbet

(works with literally any fruit;
we chose pineapple)

FOR 12 SERVINGS

1½ cups organic sugar

1½ cups water

5½ cups freshly cut ripe pineapple, about
2 pounds, or 1 large pineapple, cored and
cut into 1-inch pieces

Juice of 1 lemon (about ¼ cup)

¼ teaspoon kosher salt

1. Prep a 9 × 5-inch loaf pan by lining the entire pan with plastic wrap, pressing firmly against the bottom of the pan and up the sides and making sure there is at least 1 inch of overhang on all sides. You might need to use two sheets of plastic wrap.

2. In a medium saucepan over medium-high heat, place the sugar and water and bring to a boil, whisking constantly to ensure all the sugar is dissolved, about 1 minute. Set aside to cool.

3. Place the pineapple, lemon juice, and salt in a food processor and process until completely smooth. With the processor still running, carefully pour in the cooled sugar syrup in a steady stream and process until the mixture is evenly combined, about 20 seconds. If all the syrup won't fit in your food processor, blend half of the mixture until completely smooth, then transfer the mixture to a bowl and stir in the remaining syrup.

4. Pour the mixture into the prepared pan. Cover with plastic wrap. Freeze until solid, at least 8 hours or overnight.

5. Remove from the freezer. Let sit at room temperature for about 1 minute. Gently pull the plastic wrap from the top and then turn the pan over onto a cutting board. Gently pull on a corner of the plastic until the entire sorbet releases. Don't try to force the sorbet out or the plastic will rip; just gently pull and it will release when the sides warm up slightly. Very carefully remove the plastic wrap from the rest of the loaf. Pull the tabs to remove sorbet from the pan. With a serrated knife, cut the sorbet into roughly ½- to 1-inch cubes.

6. Add the sorbet to a food processor; depending on the size of your food processor you might need to do this in batches. Only add enough to fill the processor halfway. Pulse 25 to 30 times, scraping the sides when necessary. Once the large chunks are broken down, run the food processor on high until completely smooth. This will do two things: break down large ice crystals and whip air into the mixture. Just don't blend it for so long that the mixture turns to liquid; it should look like a slushy.

7. Pour the mixture back into the unlined loaf pan and repeat step 5 with the remaining batches if necessary. Cover with plastic wrap and freeze until set, another 4 to 5 hours. (This makes 6 cups.)

NUTRITION, per ½-cup serving

| Calories: 269 | Carbs: 70 grams | Fiber: 1 gram |
| Fat: 0 grams | Protein: 1 gram | Sugar: 65 grams |

vegan lemon poppy seed cake

V

Whether or not you follow a vegan lifestyle, this cake is definitely worth a try.

CAKE

Nonstick cooking spray

1¼ cups oat milk

Zest of 1 unwaxed lemon (about 1 tablespoon)

⅓ cup lemon juice (from about 2 lemons)

½ cup vegetable oil

1 teaspoon pure vanilla extract

1 cup organic granulated sugar

½ cup aquafaba from 1 (15-ounce) can chickpeas (see Note)

¼ teaspoon cream of tartar

2 cups whole-wheat pastry flour

1 cup all-purpose flour

1½ teaspoons baking soda

1 teaspoon baking powder

¾ teaspoon kosher salt

1½ tablespoons poppy seeds

GLAZE

1 cup organic confectioners' sugar

2 tablespoons freshly squeezed lemon juice (from ½ lemon)

Zest of 1 unwaxed lemon (about 1 tablespoon), for garnish

1. Preheat the oven to 350°F. Spray a 9-inch square cake pan with nonstick cooking spray and line the bottom with parchment paper. Spray the parchment with a little more cooking spray. Set aside.

2. In a large bowl, place the milk, lemon zest, lemon juice, oil, vanilla, and granulated sugar and whisk to combine. Set aside.

3. In a medium bowl, place the aquafaba and cream of tartar and beat on a high speed with a hand mixer or a stand mixer fitted with a whisk attachment until stiff peaks form, 5 to 6 minutes.

4. Sift the flours, baking soda, baking powder, and salt into the wet ingredients. Whisk briefly until just combined; don't overmix.

5. Add about a third of the whipped aquafaba and the poppy seeds to the batter and stir vigorously to combine and aerate the batter. Spoon in the remaining aquafaba and gently fold it into the batter to prevent deflating the aquafaba. Pour the batter into the prepared cake pan.

6. Bake until a toothpick inserted into the center comes out clean, 35 to 40 minutes. Remove the cake from the oven and let cool for 30 minutes before removing from the pan and placing the cake on a serving plate to cool completely.

7. Sift the confectioners' sugar into a medium bowl, then whisk in the lemon juice to form a glaze. Pour over the cake and garnish with the lemon zest. Serve.

NOTE

Aquafaba is the starchy liquid you've been draining out of cans of chickpeas. It's a staple in vegan cooking and baking.

NUTRITION, per serving

| Calories: 317 | Carbs: 53 grams | Fiber: 3 grams |
| Fat: 10 grams | Protein: 4 grams | Sugar: 28 grams |

grilled vanilla nectarines

FOR 4 SERVINGS

Grilled stone fruit is a perfect no-fuss dessert to cap off a summer evening. If you don't have a grill, simply sear the nectarines on the stove, then toss them in an oven preheated to 375°F until soft, about 10 minutes. This recipe works well with any stone fruit, so feel free to try this out with your favorites. Simple and fresh, this is a dish everyone will love ending their meals with.

1 vanilla bean

⅓ cup coconut sugar

2 fresh semi-ripe nectarines, halved and pits removed

¼ cup water

Vanilla ice cream or mascarpone cheese, for serving

1. Preheat a grill to medium-high for at least 20 minutes.

2. Split the vanilla bean in half. Use the back of the knife to scrape out the vanilla seeds and add them to the coconut sugar. Add the pod to the sugar as well and stir to combine.

3. Place a large flame-proof pan, such as a cast-iron skillet, on one side of the grill to preheat.

4. Place the nectarines flesh-side down on the grill. To achieve good grill marks, don't touch or fuss with them for about 4 minutes.

5. Place the nectarines in the preheated pan, flesh-side up. Sprinkle the tops of the nectarines generously with the vanilla coconut sugar, then evenly spread the rest of the sugar, including the vanilla pod, in the pan around the nectarines. Add the water to the pan and use a wooden spoon to stir the sugar and water together. Close the grill lid and cook until the nectarines have softened and the sugar water has turned into a caramel sauce, 4 to 5 minutes. Remove the vanilla bean pod and discard or compost.

6. Serve each nectarine half with a dollop of ice cream. Drizzle with the sauce from the dish.

NUTRITION, per serving (without ice cream or mascarpone topping)

| Calories: 96 | Carbs: 24 grams | Fiber: 1 gram |
| Fat: 0 grams | Protein: 1 gram | Sugar: 22 grams |

tahini black and white cookies

MAKES 14 COOKIES

You'll get both your yin and your yang in this Middle Eastern–influenced, nutty take on New York City's signature cakey cookie. This version is hearty and not too sweet. It goes seamlessly with a morning mug of hot coffee or a cup of tea. Tahini is ground sesame seeds and is a great source of calcium, iron, magnesium, and B$_1$ vitamins.

4 tablespoons (½ stick) unsalted grass-fed butter, room temperature

1 cup coconut sugar

2 large free-range eggs

1 teaspoon pure vanilla extract

1 cup tahini, mixed thoroughly before measuring

¾ cup superfine almond flour

¾ cup coconut flour

1 teaspoon baking powder

½ teaspoon kosher salt

¼ cup white sesame seeds

¼ cup black sesame seeds

1. Preheat the oven to 350°F. Line two baking sheets with reusable baking mats or parchment paper.

2. In a medium bowl with a handheld mixer, cream the butter and sugar on high until the mixture is the texture of wet sand, about 1 minute. Add the eggs and vanilla and beat until the batter is light and the beaters leave a trail behind them in the batter, 2 to 3 minutes. Add the tahini and mix until just combined.

3. Sift the flours, baking powder, and salt over the wet ingredients and mix with the hand mixer until a smooth batter forms.

4. Using a 1-ounce scoop, or a scant ¼ cup, portion out the dough and form into balls. Place the balls on the prepared baking sheets. Using a ½-cup dry measuring cup, press down on each cookie until flattened to ¼ inch thick and 3 inches in diameter.

5. To decorate, cut two 1½-inch-wide and 12-inch-long strips of parchment paper. It's best to cut from the two sides of the parchment paper so you have two edges that are perfectly straight. Add the sesame seeds to two plates or baking dishes, keeping each color separate. Wrap one parchment sheet around half a cookie and press the cookie top-side down into the black sesame seeds. Press lightly on the exposed part of the cookie to ensure the sesame seeds adhere to the cookie. Place the cookie back on the prepared baking sheet and repeat with the remaining cookies so each cookie is covered on one side with black sesame seeds. Next, wrap a new sheet of parchment over the part of the cookie that has the black sesame seeds on it and press the exposed side into the white sesame seeds. Remove the parchment and sprinkle any additional sesame seeds onto any bare parts of the cookie. Place on the baking sheets, leaving ½ inch between each cookie.

6. Bake until the edges are just starting to brown and the cookies have puffed up slightly, about 12 minutes. Remove from the oven and let cool on the baking sheet for 3 to 5 minutes before moving.

NUTRITION, per cookie

Calories: 262	Carbs: 23 grams	Fiber: 2 grams
Fat: 18 grams	Protein: 6 grams	Sugar: 14 grams

sauces

"

Our best advice for avoiding burnout while cooking wholesome dishes? Sauces.

"

feeling saucy

Looking to add some extra flavor to your food? These sauces, dips, dressings, and marinades will help! Some store-bought favorites can be loaded with salt, sugar, and a bunch of other additives. This chapter is full of flavorful yet easy alternatives that you can store in your refrigerator or freeze in ice cube trays to pull out at a moment's notice.

thai peanut sauce

MAKES ABOUT 1½ CUP

You might know this signature sauce from satay dishes at Thai restaurants. This homemade version uses only natural ingredients and still attains that complex sweet, spicy, savory, nutty flavor that goes so well with chicken, tofu, and veggies. We won't judge if you lick this right from the spoon.

½ cup unsweetened natural peanut butter

1 tablespoon Sriracha

4 teaspoons toasted sesame oil

1 tablespoon raw honey

2 tablespoons freshly squeezed lime juice

2 tablespoons water, plus more if needed

Pinch of kosher salt

1. In a medium bowl, combine the peanut butter, Sriracha, sesame oil, honey, lime juice, water, and salt. Whisk until smooth. Thin with additional water if needed to reach your desired consistency.

2. The sauce can be stored in an airtight container in the refrigerator for up to 1 week or in the freezer for up to 3 months.

NUTRITION, per 2 tablespoons

| Calories: 75 | Carbs: 4 grams | Fiber: 0 grams |
| Fat: 6 grams | Protein: 2 grams | Sugar: 2 grams |

vegan ranch

MAKES ABOUT 2 CUPS

"Vegan ranch" sounds like an oxymoron, right? Well, this recipe proves otherwise! While this ranch is dairy-free, it still has the creamy texture and tang that everyone loves. Vegan or not, you and your crew will love this!

1½ cups vegan mayonnaise

3 tablespoons unsweetened nondairy milk, plus more if needed

2 teaspoons garlic powder

1 teaspoon onion powder

½ teaspoon fine sea salt

¼ teaspoon freshly ground black pepper

¼ teaspoon paprika

1 tablespoon cider vinegar

1 teaspoon freshly squeezed lemon juice

2 teaspoons freshly chopped flat-leaf parsley, plus more for optional garnish

1 teaspoon freshly chopped dill, plus more for optional garnish

1. Place the mayo, milk, garlic powder, onion powder, salt, pepper, paprika, vinegar, and lemon juice in a blender or food processor. Blend or pulse until smooth and creamy.

2. Add the parsley and dill and pulse until well blended. The consistency at this stage is dip-like; add more milk if a dressing consistency is desirable.

3. Transfer to a small bowl or serving container and place in the refrigerator until ready to serve.

4. Garnish with more dill and parsley, if desired. Store in an airtight container in the refrigerator for up to 14 days.

NUTRITION, per 2 tablespoons

| Calories: 105 | Carbs: 4 grams | Fiber: 0 grams |
| Fat: 10 grams | Protein: 0 grams | Sugar: 2 grams |

korean-inspired sweet-and-spicy soy marinade and dressing

MAKES ABOUT 1½ CUPS

Versatility is the name of the game with this sweet, spicy, and tangy dressing. It works well with virtually anything—fish, chicken, tofu, beef, veggies, you name it! It's also a great dip for egg rolls, wontons, dumplings, and pot stickers. It's worth the effort to get the Korean red pepper powder or red chili paste, since it gives the dressing its distinctive flavor and color—it's easy to find online if you can't find it at your local grocer.

½ cup low-sodium soy sauce

2 tablespoons rice vinegar

2 tablespoons toasted sesame oil

2 tablespoons raw honey

2 tablespoons gochugaru (Korean red pepper powder) or gochujang (Korean red chili paste)

8 garlic cloves, grated (about 1 heaping tablespoon)

1 tablespoon grated fresh ginger

½ cup sliced scallions

1. In a medium bowl, combine the soy sauce, vinegar, sesame oil, honey, gochugaru, garlic, ginger, and scallions. Whisk until combined.

2. The sauce can be stored in an airtight container in the refrigerator for up to 1 week or in the freezer for up to 3 months.

NUTRITION, per 2 tablespoons

| Calories: 59 | Carbs: 8 grams | Fiber: 0 grams |
| Fat: 2 grams | Protein: 2 grams | Sugar: 4 grams |

habanero hot sauce

VG GF

MAKES ABOUT 3½ CUPS

Good news, heat seekers: you've just found your ultimate hot sauce. The capsaicin in the hot peppers used here is a miracle worker. It can boost serotonin production, reduce aches and pains, clear your sinuses, and kick-start your metabolism. And, as you might know, it's amazing on tacos, fried potatoes, eggs, and anything else, really. You'll want to have this sauce on hand at all times.

10 habanero peppers, about 4 ounces, seeded and halved

6 garlic cloves, smashed and peeled

2 tablespoons extra-virgin olive oil

2 medium carrots, diced (about 1 cup)

1 medium yellow onion, chopped (about 2 cups)

1½ teaspoons kosher salt

2 cups water

¼ cup freshly squeezed lime juice (from about 2 limes)

¼ cup white vinegar

1. Preheat the oven to 425°F. Line a baking sheet with a reusable baking mat or parchment paper.

2. Using gloves, place the habanero peppers and garlic on the baking sheet. Drizzle with 1 tablespoon of the oil and use tongs to toss to coat.

3. Roast until the edges of the peppers are brown, about 10 minutes.

4. Heat the remaining 1 tablespoon oil in a large pot over high. Add the carrots, onion, and salt. Cook, stirring constantly, until the vegetables are glossy and mostly tender, about 5 minutes.

5. Add the water, lime juice, vinegar, and roasted peppers and stir. Bring to a boil, then reduce the heat to medium-low and simmer, stirring occasionally, until the vegetables are completely tender, about 10 minutes.

6. Remove the pot from the heat and let cool.

7. Pour the mixture into a blender and purée until smooth. Use a funnel to pour the sauce into a bottle or jar, seal, and store in the refrigerator for up to 2 weeks.

NUTRITION, per 2 tablespoons

| Calories: 15 | Carbs: 2 grams | Fiber: 0 grams |
| Fat: 1 gram | Protein: 0 grams | Sugar: 1 gram |

mild jalapeño taco sauce

V GF

MAKES ABOUT 3½ CUPS

This taco sauce is a game changer. This one is mild but still has a good kick. Although *taco* is in the name, this sauce also works great outside of a tortilla. Try it on roasted cauliflower, mixed with sour cream, simmered with beans, or poured over pulled chicken or pulled pork.

1 tablespoon extra-virgin olive oil

10 jalapeños, about 10 ounces, seeded and sliced

3 garlic cloves, chopped

½ cup chopped yellow onion

1 teaspoon kosher salt

2 cups water

½ cup white vinegar

1. In a large pan, heat the olive oil over high, then add the jalapeños, garlic, onion, and salt. Cook, stirring constantly, until the vegetables are mostly tender and glossy, about 5 minutes.

2. Add the water and vinegar. Bring to a boil, then reduce the heat to medium-low and simmer, stirring occasionally, until the vegetables are completely tender, 15 to 20 minutes.

3. Remove the pan from the heat and let cool.

4. Pour the mixture into a blender and purée until smooth. Use a funnel to pour the sauce into a bottle or jar, seal, and store in the refrigerator for up to 2 months.

NUTRITION, per 2 tablespoons

| Calories: 9 | Carbs: 1 gram | Fiber: 0 grams |
| Fat: 1 gram | Protein: 0 grams | Sugar: 0 grams |

pesto, 3 ways

This tried-and-true saucy favorite has countless nutritional benefits, from possibly lowering the levels of the stress hormone cortisol to basil's liver-detoxifying properties. Pesto is great because you can switch up the herbs and nuts to fit your palate and your craving. We offer a classic basil version, one that uses spinach and walnuts, and an out-of-the-ordinary Thai-inspired pesto for when you want to spice it up.

classic pesto

MAKES ABOUT 1 CUP

2 cups lightly packed basil leaves, about 2 ounces, washed and thoroughly dried

1 garlic clove

¼ cup pine nuts, toasted

1 teaspoon kosher salt

½ teaspoon freshly ground black pepper, plus more to taste

2 to 3 tablespoons cold water

½ cup extra-virgin olive oil

½ cup freshly grated Parmesan cheese

1. Add the basil, garlic, pine nuts, salt, and pepper to a food processor and pulse about 10 times. Add the water and a splash of the oil to get things started and pulse 2 or 3 more times. Add more water to thin the mixture, if necessary. Scrape down the sides of the bowl to ensure everything is being incorporated evenly.

2. Put the top back on, turn on the food processor, and slowly drizzle the remaining oil through the feed tube until the sauce is emulsified.

3. Pour the pesto into a medium bowl, then stir in the Parmesan (the heat of the food processor motor will start to melt the cheese, so adding it afterward ensures the pesto retains a nice texture).

4. Store in an airtight container in the refrigerator for up to 1 week or in the freezer for up to 3 months.

NUTRITION, per 2 tablespoons

| Calories: 161 | Carbs: 1 gram | Fiber: 0 grams |
| Fat: 17 grams | Protein: 2 grams | Sugar: 0 grams |

spinach walnut pesto

MAKES ABOUT 1 CUP

4 cups lightly packed fresh spinach, about 4 ounces

½ cup walnuts, about 2 ounces

2 garlic cloves

½ teaspoon kosher salt

½ teaspoon freshly ground black pepper

1 tablespoon cold water

1 tablespoon freshly squeezed lemon juice

½ cup extra-virgin olive oil

¼ cup grated Parmesan cheese or nutritional yeast, about ½ ounce

1. In a food processor, place the spinach, walnuts, garlic, salt, pepper, water, and lemon juice. Pulse about 10 times, then open the lid and scrape down the sides of the bowl.

2. Replace the lid and turn on the food processor. Pour the oil in through the feed tube in a slow, steady stream and process until emulsified.

3. Pour the pesto into a medium bowl, then stir in the Parmesan.

4. Store in an airtight container in the refrigerator for up to 1 week or in the freezer for up to 3 months.

NUTRITION, per 2 tablespoons

| Calories: 178 | Carbs: 2 grams | Fiber: 1 gram |
| Fat: 19 grams | Protein: 2 grams | Sugar: 0 grams |

vegan thai basil peanut pesto

MAKES A SCANT 1 CUP

2 cups lightly packed Thai basil leaves, about 2 ounces

1 garlic clove

¼ cup dry-roasted peanuts or cashews

¼ cup toasted sesame oil

2 to 3 tablespoons cold water

½ teaspoon crushed red pepper flakes

1 tablespoon freshly squeezed lemon juice

¼ cup unsweetened shredded coconut

Kosher salt

1. Place the basil, garlic, peanuts, oil, 2 tablespoons of the water, the red pepper flakes, and the lemon juice in a food processor. Pulse 10 times, then open the lid and scrape down the sides of the bowl.

2. Add the coconut, replace the lid, and purée until smooth. Add 1 additional tablespoon of water if needed to reach your desired consistency, then season with salt.

3. Store in an airtight container in the refrigerator for up to 1 week or in the freezer for up to 3 months.

NUTRITION, per 2 tablespoons

| Calories: 107 | Carbs: 2 grams | Fiber: 1 gram |
| Fat: 11 grams | Protein: 2 grams | Sugar: 0 grams |

instant pot chicken stock, bone broth, or vegetable stock

CHICKEN STOCK AND BONE BROTH: MAKES 13 CUPS
VEGETABLE STOCK: MAKES 11½ CUPS

Make good use of leftover bones to make nutrient-rich bone broth. It can reduce inflammation, heal the gut, and protect your joints. Simply omit the bones to make veggie stock. You can sip on a cup of the stock on its own or use it as a base for soups.

3 pounds raw chicken bones (about 2 large carcasses and wings), beef bones, or pork bones

6 medium carrots, roughly chopped

6 celery stalks, roughly chopped

1 medium yellow onion, roughly chopped

4 garlic cloves, smashed and peeled

6 sprigs rosemary

6 sprigs thyme

1 tablespoon whole black peppercorns

2 tablespoons cider vinegar

12 cups cold water

1. In an Instant Pot, combine the bones, if using, the carrots, celery, onions, garlic, rosemary, thyme, peppercorns, vinegar, and water. Set the Instant Pot to HIGH SAUTÉ and bring to a boil. Once boiling, cook until any impurities foam to the surface, 8 to 10 minutes. Carefully skim the impurities from the top with a large spoon. If need be, turn off the SAUTÉ setting so the boiling subsides to make it easier to skim the impurities.

2. Place the lid on the pot and turn the VENTING valve to "sealing." Set to HIGH for 60 minutes for chicken stock or bone broth, or 30 minutes for vegetable stock.

3. Allow the Instant Pot to release pressure slowly for 15 minutes, then release the remaining pressure by switching the setting to VENTING. The hot steam will come out of the top, so make sure your hand is not over the release switch. Wait for the pressure to release completely and for the Instant Pot to unlock before removing the lid.

4. Strain the stock through a fine-mesh sieve lined with cheesecloth. Press down on the solids with a rubber spatula to release all the liquid. Let cool completely before storing in airtight containers in the refrigerator for up to 6 days or in the freezer for up to 6 months.

NOTE

Nutritional data cannot be calculated due to the vast differences in types, weights, and number of bones and vegetables used in broths.

4 whole30 dressings

The Whole30 Program is an eating style that emphasizes whole foods, focusing on fruits, veggies, and animal proteins, and omitting dairy, sugar, legumes, and anything processed. These dressings follow that philosophy, making them friendly to any dietary path. And they're totally delicious.

steps for making Whole30 dressings

1. Combine the ingredients in a mason jar and secure the lid tightly. Shake vigorously until the ingredients are mixed thoroughly.

2. Store the dressing in the refrigerator and use within 1 to 2 weeks. Shake the jar before each use.

creamy cilantro lime dressing

MAKES ABOUT 1½ CUPS

¼ cup lightly packed fresh cilantro leaves, finely chopped

Kosher salt and freshly ground black pepper

½ cup full-fat unsweetened coconut milk, mixed well before measuring

¼ cup freshly squeezed lime juice (from about 2 limes)

½ cup avocado oil or extra-virgin olive oil

NUTRITION, per 2 tablespoons

Calories: 121	Carbs: 1 gram	Fiber: 0 grams
Fat: 13 grams	Protein: 0 grams	Sugar: 0 grams

garlic-ginger "soy" dressing

1 tablespoon minced garlic

1 tablespoon minced fresh ginger

Kosher salt and freshly ground black pepper

2 tablespoons toasted sesame oil

¼ cup rice vinegar

½ cup extra-virgin olive oil

½ cup coconut aminos

NUTRITION, per 2 tablespoons

| Calories: 121 | Carbs: 2 grams | Fiber: 0 grams |
| Fat: 11 grams | Protein: 0 grams | Sugar: 2 grams |

raspberry balsamic dressing

MAKES ABOUT 1¾ CUPS

1 tablespoon Dijon mustard

½ cup raspberries, about 2 ounces, puréed

¼ cup freshly squeezed lemon juice

¼ cup red wine vinegar

¼ cup balsamic vinegar

½ cup extra-virgin olive oil

NUTRITION, per 2 tablespoons

| Calories: 89 | Carbs: 2 grams | Fiber: 0 grams |
| Fat: 9 grams | Protein: 0 grams | Sugar: 1 gram |

herby italian dressing

MAKES ABOUT 2 CUPS

1 tablespoon minced garlic

1 tablespoon lightly packed finely chopped fresh oregano leaves

2 tablespoons lightly packed finely chopped fresh flat-leaf parsley leaves

1 tablespoon lightly packed finely chopped fresh basil leaves

Kosher salt and freshly ground black pepper

¾ cup white wine vinegar

1 cup extra-virgin olive oil

NUTRITION, per 2 tablespoons

| Calories: 123 | Carbs: 0 grams | Fiber: 0 grams |
| Fat: 14 grams | Protein: 0 grams | Sugar: 0 grams |

3 sweet syrups

Make these wholesome simple syrups to have on hand for mixing into cocktails and other drinks or for drizzling over cakes, ice cream, yogurt, fruit, pancakes . . . wherever you crave a little more sweetness. No worries, though—these syrups get their sugar content from pure, all-natural sources.

pomegranate molasses

MAKES ABOUT 1 CUP

4 cups 100% pure pomegranate juice

1 cup coconut sugar

1. Place the pomegranate juice and sugar in a large saucepan over high heat. Bring to a boil, stirring constantly until the sugar dissolves.

2. Lower the heat to medium and simmer until the juice is reduced to about 1 cup, 50 to 60 minutes. The syrup should be thick enough to coat the back of a spoon but will continue to thicken as it cools. Set aside to cool to room temperature, about 1 hour.

3. Store in an airtight container in the refrigerator for up to 6 months.

NUTRITION, per 2 tablespoons

| Calories: 160 | Carbs: 40 grams | Fiber: 0 grams |
| Fat: 0 grams | Protein: 0 grams | Sugar: 40 grams |

orange ginger honey syrup

MAKES ABOUT 1½ CUPS

¾ cup water

¾ cup raw honey

1½ inches fresh ginger, thinly sliced

1 large navel orange

1. Place the water, honey, and ginger in a small saucepan over medium heat. Heat until simmering, stirring to ensure the honey is completely dissolved, about 1 minute. Remove from the heat.

2. Use a vegetable peeler to zest the orange into long strips. Add the zest to the hot honey and stir. Let cool to room temperature, about 1 hour.

3. Strain the syrup. As the syrup cools it will thicken slightly. If a thicker syrup is desired, put it back over medium heat and reduce to your desired consistency.

4. The syrup will keep in an airtight container in the refrigerator for up to 1 month. It tastes great on pancakes, waffles, and muffins, or in tea or cocktails.

NUTRITION, per 2 tablespoons

| Calories: 52 | Carbs: 14 grams | Fiber: 0 grams |
| Fat: 0 grams | Protein: 0 grams | Sugar: 13 grams |

date syrup

1 cup pitted Medjool dates (about 13 dates)

2 teaspoons freshly squeezed lemon juice

⅛ teaspoon kosher salt

1½ cups hot water, plus more as needed

1. In a high-speed blender, place the dates, lemon juice, and salt. Carefully pour in the hot water and allow to soak for about 15 minutes.

2. Blend the dates on high until totally smooth (there will still be small specks of date visible), about 1 minute. Add more water as needed to reach your desired consistency.

3. Store in an airtight container in the refrigerator for up to 2 weeks.

NUTRITION, per 2 tablespoons

| Calories: 35 | Carbs: 9 grams | Fiber: 1 gram |
| Fat: 0 grams | Protein: 0 grams | Sugar: 8 grams |

vinegar barbecue sauce

MAKES ABOUT 3 CUPS

This barbecue sauce is a mix between the sweet classic sauce and a Carolina vinegar-based barbecue sauce. It's low in sugar without sacrificing flavor. (Because what's the point of a barbecue sauce without flavor?!) Pour it on chicken and ribs or slather it on sandwiches.

1½ teaspoons avocado oil

½ yellow onion, grated (about ½ cup)

2 garlic cloves, minced

1 teaspoon kosher salt, plus more to taste

1 teaspoon freshly ground black pepper

2 cups cider vinegar

½ cup molasses

½ cup coconut sugar

½ cup ketchup

¼ cup tamari

½ teaspoon cayenne pepper

1½ teaspoons mustard powder

1. In a medium saucepan over medium heat, stir together in the oil, onion, garlic, salt, and pepper. Cook until the onion begins to caramelize and the pepper is toasted and fragrant, about 5 minutes.

2. Add the vinegar, molasses, sugar, ketchup, tamari, cayenne, and mustard powder. Bring to a boil and then simmer, stirring constantly to ensure the sugar is completely dissolved, until the sauce reduces to about 3 cups and is thick enough to coat the back of a spoon, 10 to 12 minutes. Remove from the heat and cool to room temperature. Season with salt.

3. Pour the sauce into a jar or bottle and seal. Store in the refrigerator for up to 2 weeks.

NUTRITION, per ¼ cup

| Calories: 88 | Carbs: 19 grams | Fiber: 0 grams |
| Fat: 1 gram | Protein: 1 gram | Sugar: 17 grams |

2-minute homemade mayo and 3 mix-ins for "aioli"

EACH RECIPE MAKES ABOUT ⅔ CUP

Yes, you can make your own fresh mayonnaise, and it'll be more nutritious than any store-bought one. It's best made with an immersion blender, but you can use a blender or an electric hand mixer instead. If using a blender or hand mixer, first mix everything but the oil and then slowly add the oil teaspoon by teaspoon until it starts to emulsify. Finally, drizzle in the remaining oil in a slow, steady stream. Use our recommended mix-ins for standout flavors or choose any other one you can think of.

BASIC MAYO

1 large free-range egg yolk, room temperature

1 teaspoon Dijon mustard

1 teaspoon white wine vinegar (cider or distilled white work too)

1½ teaspoons freshly squeezed lemon juice

¼ teaspoon kosher salt

⅔ cup olive oil (not extra-virgin) or another mild-tasting oil

1. In a mason jar, place the egg yolk, mustard, vinegar, lemon juice, salt, and oil. If you're flavoring your mayonnaise, add the flavoring ingredients now. Set aside until the oil rises completely to the top, about 1 minute.

2. Push an immersion blender to the bottom of the jar and blend, ensuring the blender stays in contact with the bottom of the jar, until all the

ingredients under the oil is emulsified. Then begin to incorporate the oil slowly until evenly combined and the mayonnaise is white and fluffy, about 1 minute.

lemon garlic

1 small garlic clove

Zest of ½ unwaxed lemon (about 1½ teaspoons)

chipotle

1 to 2 tablespoons adobo sauce, depending on desired heat level

three-herb

1½ teaspoons loosely packed freshly chopped basil leaves

1½ teaspoons loosely packed freshly chopped thyme leaves

1½ teaspoons loosely packed freshly chopped tarragon leaves

NUTRITION, per 2 tablespoons Basic Mayo

Calories: 135	Carbs: 0 grams	Fiber: 0 grams
Fat: 15 grams	Protein: 0 grams	Sugar: 0 grams

shopping lists for prep recipes

(pages 60–83)

Note: Lists assume salt and pepper is on hand.

ROASTED CAULIFLOWER AND CURRY SOUP

Produce

1 medium head cauliflower

1 small yellow onion

1 jalapeño

2 garlic cloves

Oils and Liquids

Coconut oil

4 cups vegetable stock

Nuts and Seeds

½ cup raw pepitas, about 2½ ounces

Canned Goods

3 tablespoons red curry paste

1 (14-ounce) can unsweetened coconut milk

Seasonings

Curry powder

Garlic powder

Onion powder

Optional

Scallions, for serving

Fresh cilantro, for serving

Lime wedges, for serving

BROILED CHICKEN SHAWARMA WITH GARLICKY WHITE SAUCE

Produce

1 unwaxed lemon

4 garlic cloves

Meat

2 pounds boneless, skinless chicken thighs

Dairy

1 cup whole-milk Greek yogurt, about 8 ounces

Oils and Liquids

Extra-virgin olive oil

Seasonings

Cumin

Ground cardamom

Paprika

Cinnamon

Ground turmeric

Garlic powder

Ground sumac

Cayenne pepper

FREEZER-PREP MUSHROOM AND CHICKEN BURRITOS

Produce

½ yellow onion

1½ pounds mixed mushrooms, such as cremini, shiitake, and king oyster

⅓ cup cilantro

1 lime

Meat

2 boneless, skinless chicken breasts, about 12 ounces

Dairy

1½ cups low-sodium Mexican-blend shredded cheese, about 3½ ounces

Oils and Liquids

Avocado oil

Canned Goods

½ cup jarred salsa

1 (16-ounce) can low-sodium refried black beans

Grains and Bread

6 (10-inch) multigrain low-carb tortillas

1½ cups cooked brown rice, about 9 ounces

Seasonings

Cumin

Chili powder

Garlic powder

HONEY-MUSTARD CHICKEN WITH ROASTED BRUSSELS SPROUTS

Produce

1 medium sweet potato

About 6 ounces red potatoes

1 small red onion

About 3½ ounces Brussels sprouts

About 4 ounces green beans

1 large carrot

3 garlic cloves

Fresh thyme

Fresh rosemary

Meat

4 bone-in, skin-on chicken thighs, about 2 pounds

Oils and Liquids

Extra-virgin olive oil

¼ cup Dijon mustard

¼ cup raw honey

TERIYAKI EDAMAME TURKEY MEATBALLS

Produce

About 4½ ounces frozen shelled edamame

5 scallions

4 garlic cloves

1 small knob fresh ginger

About 2 cups snow peas

Meat

1 pound 93% lean ground turkey

Eggs/Dairy

1 large free-range egg

Oils and Liquids

¾ cup low-sodium tamari

2 tablespoons raw honey

¼ cup rice wine vinegar

Dry Goods

½ cup crispy brown rice cereal or panko

1½ teaspoons cornstarch

BUFFALO CHICKPEA GRAIN BOWLS

Produce

1 medium yellow onion

2 garlic cloves

1 carrot

2 celery stalks

5 small radishes

Oils and Liquids

3 cups low-sodium vegetable stock

2 tablespoons avocado oil

2 tablespoons cider vinegar

½ cup low-sodium hot sauce

Canned and Dry Goods

1 tablespoon coconut sugar

2 (15-ounce) cans no-salt-added chickpeas

1 tablespoon tomato paste

Grains

1½ cups farro, about 9½ ounces

Seasonings

Paprika

Cumin

Cayenne pepper (optional)

SLOW-COOKER ROASTED TOMATO AND BASIL SOUP

Produce

2 pounds Roma or vine-ripened tomatoes (about 8 tomatoes)

1 red bell pepper

1 medium yellow onion

6 garlic cloves

½ cup fresh basil leaves

Oils and Liquids

½ cup extra-virgin olive oil

2 cups low-sodium vegetable stock

Canned Goods

1 tablespoon tomato paste

Seasonings

Oregano

Thyme

BALSAMIC SOY SALMON AND VEGGIE BAKE

Produce

2 garlic cloves

1 large carrot

5 ounces green beans

5 ounces asparagus

1 medium yellow squash

Meat

4 (6-ounce) skin-on salmon fillets

Oils and Liquids

¼ cup soy sauce

¼ cup balsamic vinegar

1½ tablespoons extra-virgin olive oil

Seasonings

Paprika

Garlic powder

Onion powder

INSTANT POT CHIPOTLE CARNITAS

Produce

2 medium yellow onions

1 carrot

1 garlic head

1 orange

Meat

2½ pounds pork shoulder

Oils and Liquids

1 tablespoon avocado oil

Canned Goods

1 (7-ounce) can chipotles in adobo sauce

Seasonings

Cumin

Ground coriander

Bay leaves

acknowledgments

A massive thank-you to everyone who contributes to Goodful!

MARKETING

Alana Tabak
Amal Mgaresh
Benedict Leung
Chelsea Portner
Emily DePaula
Emily Jax
Eric Karp
Jessica Seib
Josie Fox
Julia Queller
Michelle Sullivan
Nilla Ali
Parker Ortolani
Shira Mahler
Talia Halperin

DESIGN AND ILLUSTRATION

Devon McGowan
Ivy Tai
Michael Kilian
Nina Patane

RECIPE DEVELOPMENT

Claire King

RECIPE TESTING

Ali Clarke
Carrie Hildebrand
Claire King
Karlee Rotoly
Susan Vu
Talia Goldstein

WRITING

Alana Tabak
Lisa DeFazio

SOCIAL

David Bertozzi
Emma Tyler
Irash Osmanzada
Janna Macatangay
Skylar Kearney

PRODUCERS

Alexandra Addison
Crystal Hatch
Ellyse O'Halloran
Erin VanSloten
Jessica Massa
John Gannon
Maycie Timpone
Merle O'Neal
Nadia Honary
Natalie Ullman
Peggy Wang
Rachel Gaewski
Ramon Flores
Spencer Kombol
Tarn Susumpow
Tiffany Lo
Trish Lindo

ADVERTISING AND PARTNERSHIPS

Augusta Falletta
Brittany Zar

Emily Erhart
Jay Anandpara
Justine Teu
Kathryn Schmidbauer
Lindsay Stanislau
Michelle Corbolotti
Nicole Ngo
Sundy He

BRANDED CREATIVE

Alexandra Schlagel
Carol Tan
Hannah Williams
Jessica Jardine
Kate Gnetetsky
Matt Mandarino
Samra Seifu
Swasti Shukla
Tracy Raetz

TECH

Edgar Sanchez
Jess Anastasio
Kate Zasada
Kiyana Salkeld

OPERATIONS

Emily Favilla
Laina Kaffenberger
Marshall Pease
Michael Chavez
Nicole Agredano
Rebecca Magenheim
Troy Brady

index